D0996878

A MASTER'S GUIDE TO

Atlantic Salmon Fishing

A MASTER'S GUIDE TO
Atlantic Salmon Fishing

BILL CUMMINGS

RAGGED MOUNTAIN PRESS

CAMDEN, MAINE

Published by Ragged Mountain Press

10 9 8 7 6 5 4 3 2 1

Library of Congress Cataloging-in-Publication Data
Cummings, Bill.
A master's guide to Atlantic salmon fishing / Bill Cummings :
contributors to chapter 11, Bob Baker . . . [et. al.]
p. cm.
Includes bibliographic references (p. 214) and index.
ISBN 0-07-015059-1
1. Atlantic Salmon fishing. 2. Atlantic Salmon fishing--Canada, Eastern. I. Title.
SH685.C85 1995   95-10516
799.1'755--dc20   CIP

Questions regarding the content of this book should be addressed to:
Ragged Mountain Press
P.O. Box 220
Camden, ME 04843

Questions regarding the ordering of this book should be addressed to:
McGraw-Hill, Inc.
Customer Service Department
P.O. Box 547
Blacklick, OH 43004
Retail Customers: 1-800-822-8158
Bookstores: 1-800-722-4726

For every book sold, Ragged Mountain Press will make a donation to an environmental cause.

 A Master's Guide to Atlantic Salmon Fishing is printed on recycled paper containing a minimum of 50% total recycled paper with 10% postconsumer de-inked fiber.

Printed by R.R. Donnelley, Crawfordsville, Indiana
Design by Ann Aspell
Illustrations by Dan Daly
Color photos by William Thuss
Production by Molly Mulhern
Edited by James R. Babb, George V. Roberts Jr.
Contributors to Chapter 11: Bob Baker, Kenneth Beland, Dick Brown, Bill Bryson, Ephraim Massey, and Len Rich.

TO PHYLLIS

CONTENTS

Color plates of salmon flies and their patterns appear following page 112.

FOREWORD

by Lefty Kreh

This is a book about Atlantic salmon fishing by someone who has spent a lifetime chasing this marvelous fish. Bill Cummings is not an experienced outdoor writer or someone who wants to be "recognized" by writing a book. Instead, Bill is just your regular guy who has been lucky enough to fish many of the fine Atlantic salmon waters.

Bill and I fished New Zealand together, where our in-the-boat conversations convinced me that he had much to share with those interested in the salmon. His casting and fish-catching techniques showed me he has pretty well mastered the sport. Did he ever think about putting his ideas on paper?, I asked. His face wrinkled in a big smile as he answered, "I've written a book on the subject."

He sent me the manuscript, and it's good! There are many subtle techniques here that pay off.

Many scientific experiments show that 80 percent of the fishermen catch about 10 percent of the fish. This applies to fresh and salt water, and to trout, salmon, bass, and almost all species. Another way of stating the results of the surveys is that about 20 percent (or fewer) of all anglers catch nearly 90 percent of the fish. After spending time with Bill and reading his manuscript, I'm convinced he belongs in that enviable 20 percent circle.

Bill is quiet but very observant. His book represents a lifetime of fishing for the Atlantic salmon by someone who obviously loves the sport. Anyone who shares this love will enjoy this book.

ACKNOWLEDGMENTS

Some of the ideas in this book have their origins in conversations with other salmon anglers, now deceased. To say who had the seminal thought, or who contributed the greater part of its substance, would be impossible, especially at this late date. The best I can do is to recognize the contributions of these astute anglers, and to express my regrets that their passing has deprived me of their companionship and their long experience in dealing with salmon: Sharp Pond, Cole Wilde, Father Elmer J. Smith, and Herb McKay. Thank you, gentlemen, for stimulating my thinking and correcting me when I got off on the wrong track.

Orvid Clark has fished with me for more than 30 years. He and his wife, Inez, tolerated my idiosyncrasies and my chronic inability to land a grilse for the pot over many seasons at their camp. These were very happy times. They also provided me the opportunity to examine salmon-fishing concepts over a long enough time span to get a meaningful idea of their validity.

Jim Babb and Tom McCarthy guided this first-time book author through the complexities of the publishing process with expertise, patience, and goodwill. Now if they will go out and catch a salmon I'll consider the whole enterprise a success.

Ron Rogstad always made himself available in a variety of ways, often as a sounding board for the clarity of my expression. Although Ron hasn't made it to the salmon rivers at this writing, he is an excellent fly-fisher and could tell me when my writing failed to make things clear without my having to explain fly-fishing terms.

Parts of Chapters 6, 7, and 11 first appeared in the *Atlantic Salmon Journal*. My thanks to Harry Bruce, its editor-in-chief, for permission to use them here.

The excellent photograph of a salmon's scale was contributed by Dr. Geoff Power of the University of Waterloo. My interpretation of it is based largely on his article, which appeared in the Winter 1987 *Atlantic Salmon Journal*.

John Randolph, editor of *Fly Fisherman*, kindly gave permission to reproduce the maps of the Atlantic salmon's ocean migrations.

Gary LaFontaine generously allowed me to quote extensively from his fine book *The Dry Fly: New Angles*. His theory relating the color of incident light to the effectiveness of trout flies brought to mind enough incidents in my experience to suggest an extension of the concept to salmon fishing.

I am indebted to Jerry Doak of W.W. Doak & Sons, the fine fly shop in Doaktown, New Brunswick, for providing the following flies shown in the color plates: Undertaker, Shady Lady, Rusty Rat, Cosseboom, Mickey Finn, Oriole, Butterfly, Green Highlander, Rat-Faced MacDougall, White Wulff, MacIntosh, and Whiskers. These are easily distinguished by their superior quality from the others pictured (for which I am responsible).

Kenneth Beland kindly permitted me to reprint his article on salmon fishing in Maine, which first appeared in *Maine Fish and Wildlife Magazine*.

I've used comments on salmon rods and leaders from Edward R. Hewitt's book *A Trout and Salmon Fisherman for Seventy-Five Years*, copyright 1948, by Charles Scribner's Sons.

Brief quotations from Eric Taverner's *Salmon Fishing* were the antecedents of my remarks on the influence of color on salmon-fly attraction. I extend my thanks to Pen & Sword Books Limited for permission to use them.

Figures from the Jock Scott book on greased-line fishing aided my presentation of that subject. I thank Frank Amato of Amato Publications for his permission to reproduce them.

My appreciation to L. James Bashline for permission to use the drawings of the Portland hitch that appeared in his book *Atlantic Salmon Fishing*.

INTRODUCTION

A fly-fisher receives a telephone call from his longtime guide, who tells him the Atlantic salmon run is underway on New Brunswick's Miramichi River. The angler calls a friend, and by that evening they are on their way north, driving all night to be on the scene as soon as possible.

A woman sits on a roadside bluff overlooking a pool on Quebec's Matane River. Down below, an angler covers the pool systematically with a wet fly. The woman has been sitting there eight or more hours a day for over a week, waiting for her husband to get his fill of salmon fishing.

A dentist begins salmon fishing for only a week each season. As the years go on, however, he gradually pares down his summer appointment schedule until he is fishing for salmon all season long.

Ira Gruber came to the Miramichi area for the hunting. While there, he tried salmon fishing and found it so much to his liking he eventually built a house near the river to accommodate his family, and was soon fishing every day of the season, year after year.

Father Elmer Smith filled in for a vacationing priest whose parish was on the banks of the Miramichi River. He became so involved with salmon fishing he eventually moved to Canada and stayed there the rest of his life.

If you are a trout angler you can somewhat understand these rather extreme reactions to what is, after all, a recreational activity. You know the pleasure of fly-casting on a May day when the insects are active, the river clear and cool, and the trout hungry. But to cause this kind of extreme behavior, fly-fishing for salmon must involve other things.

Indeed it does. First, the smallest salmon you are likely to catch will weigh 3 to 6 pounds (1.36 to 2.72 kilograms)—a trophy on most trout anglers' scales. The average salmon will be in the 8- to 12-pound range (3.6 to 5.4 kilograms), with the possibility of picking up a much larger fish. While fish of this size may be available to saltwater fly-anglers, the dedicated trouter longs for the ambiance of an unspoiled, free-flowing river.

Along with horse racing, salmon fishing has long been the sport of kings. Traditionally, Europe's prime salmon waters were reserved for royalty, while its lesser rivers were controlled by the landed gentry. To this day, sections of the River Dee, near Balmoral Castle in Scotland, are reserved exclusively for British royalty. Historically, the salmon represented a source of food to the royal subjects, who did not hesitate to exercise what they considered their rights to the fish by poaching on "milord's river."

In North America, reaction to the British tradition maintained that all salmon waters should be open to the public. This arrangement soon lost any significance in the United States, since it took only a century for dams, pollution, and commercial fishing to bring the Atlantic salmon to the brink of extinction. By the turn of the century it was necessary to cross the border into Quebec or the Maritime Provinces to find quality salmon fishing. Due to the expense and time involved in the trek by train, wagon, and canoe, this was not an option for the common man. And men of wealth found the fishing quality diminished by subsistence and commercial netting in the estuaries and rivers. Their solution was to approach the Provincial Governments and secure leases for the fishing rights on the rivers, and then hire guardians to ward off all would-be netters and poachers. To fund this, they usually set up a corporation, charging each shareholder an annual fee to defray the cost of leasing and maintaining the property and to pay the wages of the guardians.

From a conservational standpoint, having these private clubs control the prime salmon water was an ideal situation. Netting was all but eliminated in the estuaries and rivers, and the relatively few fish taken by the anglers were no threat to the stock. However, this arrangement restricted the use of the resource to the wealthy.

With the development of the automobile came increased pressure to make salmon fishing available to those of more modest means. Fishing access was made increasingly available through outfitters, who provided lodging and guide service on the unleased waters. For anglers willing to fish rotation on the limited public water, it was possible, on a few rivers, to rent a room nearby, further reducing costs.

Each winter, Quebec holds a telephone lottery through which fishing rights on public waters are made available. Quebec also has local administrative organizations called ZECs, which regulate individual rivers (this is detailed in Chapter 11).

I began salmon fishing in 1958 at the Jack Russell Camps (then owned by Eldred Bailey) on the Miramichi River in Ludlow, New Brunswick. After a few trips to Maine's Machias River, I made yearly trips, from 1960 to 1978, to the Matane River on Quebec's Gaspé Peninsula. Three times during that period I got in some time on Scotland's South Esk. Upon retiring in 1984, I have been able to spend a good deal more time salmon fishing at a private camp on the Miramichi. In 1991 I also spent a week with Ken Gray at his camps on the Nepisiguit River, north of the Miramichi.

I present this short list of rivers to inform the reader that this book will not, for the most part, deal with exotic locations and the relatively easy fishing they sometimes provide. The Matane was overfished with increasing severity throughout the 1970s. By the 1980s the Miramichi stock was so depleted by commercial netting that there was serious question whether it would survive. Fish seldom came easily on these waters. The competition for pools on the Matane increased sharply as the river became better known (the daily permit, which ballooned from $4 to $25, did nothing to discourage anglers). This might be called the "tough" fishing for Atlantic salmon. This is where most of the new approaches have been developed, and where, I suspect, we shall see most future developments. This tough salmon fishing and its resulting developments are the subjects of this book.

The Atlantic salmon is *anadromous*, which means its life is divided between a freshwater and saltwater existence. From the time it leaves the ocean as an adult on its spawning run, it does not feed. The migration upriver involves heavy currents, rapids, and waterfalls. Any fish not capable of storing sufficient energy to surmount these obstacles is eliminated from contributing to the evolutionary process. As a result we have today's *Salmo salar*, a fish of incomparable strength and vitality. It was named *salar*—"the leaper"—by the Roman Legions, who encountered it in every sizable stream in Northern Europe.

In terms of casting and wading, trout-fishing experience is useful in pursuing salmon. The quarry, however, is distinctly different and will require quite different tactics. If you attempt to fish for salmon as you do for trout, reading the water to present your flies to feeding stations, you are on the wrong track, for the salmon are not feeding. If you watch other salmon anglers, you will find they congregate at specific locations—the pools—and pay absolutely no attention to the long stretches in between, which to the trout angler look magnificent. Watch these experienced anglers an hour or more and it will seem they spend a long time covering the pools with little to show for their efforts.

As time goes on, they seem to spend more time changing flies and discussing the situation than they do fishing. You are sure there are salmon present, for you have seen them jump several times while you've been watching. Since salmon returning to spawn in the rivers are not known to eat anything, the angler's lack of success in enticing them to take flies, which simulate food, would hardly seem surprising. The angler must hope that the salmon's urge to eat is not completely turned off, even though food now serves no useful purpose to the fish. How best to excite a flickering appetite is both the challenge of salmon fishing and, on a successful day, one of its great rewards.

Compared with Pacific salmons and other gamefishes, fishing for Atlantic salmon is much more difficult. Playing a salmon requires skills and judgments not needed for most trout-fishing situations (the notable exception is fly-fishing for steelhead, which has many similarities to Atlantic-salmon fishing). Additional challenges arise from the salmon's inconsistent behavior. Never use the words *never* or *always* when discussing this fish's behavior! Typically the salmon takes a fly with a great pull, but at times it will nip at it. At times it will demand a large fly and at other times a small one. Now the fly must be bright and another time it must be dull. Sometimes the fish cannot be tempted at all. The salmon reacts to the water temperature and height—but not consistently. Over the years, a good deal of lore has been generated by salmon anglers attempting to deal with these vagaries—most of which has so many exceptions as to be virtually useless.

Why then bother to fish for salmon? For many the answer lies in the magnificence of the fish and the fascination with developing new insights to provide a better chance of bringing them to our flies. With a no-kill policy in place on most salmon rivers comes an additional reward: To assist the fish in recovering from the fight and swim off toward the spawning beds provides many anglers with much greater satisfaction than did the bloody landings of yesteryear.

Considering all the natural hazards the salmon encounters, it seems most inappropriate that man should belabor the fish with pollution, dams, nets, siltation, poaching, and yes, angling. I can only justify the last by arguing that the Atlantic salmon would have become extinct long ago had it not been for the sport angler, who has been its constant champion.

With buyouts of commercial fishing quotas, such as those in Newfoundland and Iceland, the resurgence of Atlantic salmon returning to most rivers has been encouraging and in some cases phenomenal—and we can expect further improvement. The campaign to declare the Atlantic salmon an endangered species in the United States, I feel, is ill-advised, for without anglers on the rivers serious poaching would ensue.

(Before your first cast, note that regulations governing the taking of Atlantic salmon change frequently and vary from one area to the next. Always check with the appropriate authorities on license restrictions. In general, the taking of salmon exceeding 24.8 inches [63cm], measured from the tip of its snout to the fork of its tail, is prohibited in Canada. Fish less than 24.8 inches in length (grilse) may be retained if tagged, but tagging restrictions and limits vary from province to province. Maine has a seasonal limit of 1 Atlantic salmon, with special regulations limiting the number of salmon longer than 25 inches that can be taken from certain rivers.)

I propose in this book to examine some of the problems peculiar to Atlantic salmon fishing. The answers provided by other authors will in some cases be compared with and tested against my own experiences and the experiences of those who have fished with me and have influenced my thinking. I hope to emphasize the disparity of thought on these subjects, and to point out the dangers of accepting the lore of the sport uncritically. This is not to say you should approach salmon fishing thoughtlessly—the all-too-common chuck-and-chance-it method. Experience will suggest how best to fish under the conditions at hand and, based on your ongoing observations, how to modify your approach as you proceed.

CHAPTER I

Life History of the Atlantic Salmon

It is scarcely possible to doubt that the varieties
of the salmon which haunt the sea, come to the
same rivers to breed in which they were born,
or where they have spawned before.

—Sir Humphrey Davy, *Salmonia*

S IR HUMPHREY DAVY WAS A RENOWNED NINETEENTH-CENTURY CHEMIST and ardent fly-angler. In 1828 he published a book titled *Salmonia*, in which (writing as Halieus or Hal.) he tells of pursuing fishes of the family Salmonidae: trout, salmon, and grayling. He writes in the preface: "The conversational manner and discursive style was chosen as best suited to the state of health of the author, who was incapable of considerable efforts and long continued attention; and he could not but have in mind a model, which has fully proved the utility and popularity of this method of treating the subject, *The Compleat Angler* of Walton and Cotton."

Salmonia tells us how salmon fishing was conducted in early-nineteenth-century England. It also serves to remind us how little we have learned in the intervening century and a half.

EGGS, ALEVINS, FRY, FINGERLINGS

The Atlantic salmon's complex life history is one of the marvels of the natural world. It comprises several years of river life, a complete adaptation to life at sea, and a poorly understood migration across thousands of miles of the North Atlantic to return to its native river to spawn and thus begin the cycle anew.

Fertilized salmon eggs, which are buried 6 to 12 inches (15 to 30 centimeters) in the river gravel by the female in the fall, hatch out the following spring in response to the warming water. The hatchlings, called *alevins* at this stage, are protected from predation by the surrounding gravel. They are about ½ inch (1.3 centimeters) long and cannot move very well due to their relatively large yolk sac (Figure 1-1). Until they are about a month old, this yolk is their only food.

By early summer the young fish emerge from the protective gravel and begin swimming about, feeding on microscopic organisms. They are now known as *fry*. The fry grow rapidly, and on attaining a length of 1 inch (2.5 centimeters) are called *fingerlings*. They retain this designation until they exceed the length of a finger, after which they are referred to as *parr*.

PARR AND THE RIVER LIFE

At this stage the young salmon develop the characteristic parr markings: a series of 8 to 11 dark blotches on either side of their body. Otherwise, their appearance is quite similar to that of small brown trout. Parr remain in the river from two to

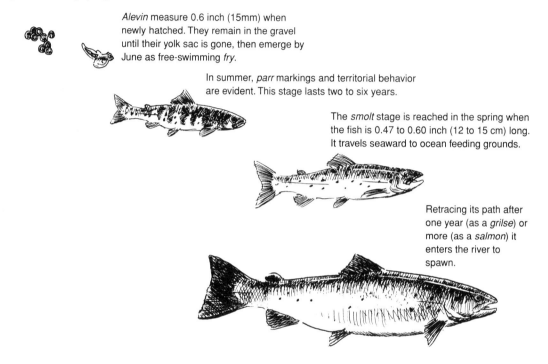

In late fall, fertilized eggs are deposited in a streambed *redd*. The adult fish, now *kelt*, return to the sea. They may spawn again one to two years later. An average 9 pound (4 kg) female may lay 8,000 eggs. These incubate deep in the gravel until early spring.

Alevin measure 0.6 inch (15mm) when newly hatched. They remain in the gravel until their yolk sac is gone, then emerge by June as free-swimming *fry*.

In summer, *parr* markings and territorial behavior are evident. This stage lasts two to six years.

The *smolt* stage is reached in the spring when the fish is 0.47 to 0.60 inch (12 to 15 cm) long. It travels seaward to ocean feeding grounds.

Retracing its path after one year (as a *grilse*) or more (as a *salmon*) it enters the river to spawn.

FIGURE 1.1. *Life cycle of the Atlantic salmon.*

as many as eight years. Predation during this period by eels and other fishes, as well as by kingfishers, ducks, and other birds is heavy, but is balanced by the henfish's producing an average of 800 eggs per pound (0.45 kilogram) of body weight (though about half these eggs are lost during the winter).

The parr is a marvelous athlete. Spotting an insect flying low over the river, it will leap clear of the water as much as 2 feet (0.6 meter)—about five times its length—to catch it. Seeing an angler's dry fly on the surface, it will attack it viciously and repeatedly from all angles to drown what appears to be a piece of food. Parr are often caught on wet flies as well. Release all parr by holding the hook shank firmly and allowing them to wriggle free, thereby avoiding damage to their protective mucous coating.

The parr feeds similarly to a small trout. Major feeding times are in the early morning and late evening, corresponding with the times of the major hatches. It offers reassurance to the angler casting for mature salmon to see the pool surface covered with the dimples of rising parr. Although only a few percent will survive to return as adults, it is critical that the river hold the maximum number of parr sustainable. The parr's feeding is greatly inhibited by strong light and by water temperatures exceeding 75 degrees F (24 degrees C).

SMOLTS AND THEIR IMPRINTING

Upon attaining a critical size (an average length of 5.35 inches or 13.6 centimeters), the parr undergoes a transformation to become what is known as a *smolt*. The most obvious change is the disappearance of the parr markings, which are replaced by a silvery hue (Figure 1-1). Also, the tail lengthens and becomes more deeply forked. At the same time, hormonal changes prepare the fish for the move from fresh water to salt. Another change of particular importance is called *imprinting*, whereby the fish memorizes the odor of its home stream and can recognize it on its return as the stream's waters are washed into the sea by the spring spates.

This salmon-homing mechanism was proven by experiments conducted in the 1950s by A.D. Hasler and A.T. Scholz on coho (silver) salmon. Hasler and Scholz found they could imprint salmon by substituting certain organic chemicals for the natural odors of rivers. In a typical experiment, one group of coho smolts was held in hatchery water containing a trace of morpholine (MOR), while another group was exposed to a minute amount of phenethyl alcohol (PEA); a third control group was kept in unadulterated water. Each fish was fin-clipped so it could be identified as a member of a particular group. All the smolts were then released about halfway between two spawning streams entering Lake Michigan. After a year and a half, when the spawning migration of these fish was about to begin, MOR was released into one of the streams and PEA into the other. The fin-clipped fish were identified after they were caught by anglers or were immobilized by electroshocking. In the MOR stream, 95 percent of the fin-clipped fish were MOR-imprinted; in the PEA stream, 92.5 percent of those with clipped fins were PEA-imprinted. The unimprinted control fish were widely scattered. Similar experiments have shown that Atlantic salmon are imprinted in the same way as cohos.

The length of time it takes for a parr to become a smolt is determined by the feeding opportunities of the natal river. The critical size can be attained in as little as one year in the southernmost part of the fish's range, where the feeding season is long, but it may require as many as six to eight years in the northernmost regions. To prepare for their long sea journey, the smolts feed vigorously and opportunistically during their descent of the river.

LIFE AT SEA AND THE RETURN TO THE RIVERS

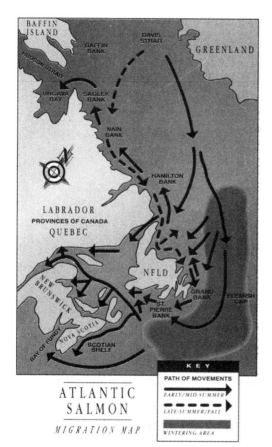

ATLANTIC
SALMON

MIGRATION MAP

FIGURE 1-2. *Migration routes of North American Atlantic salmon.*

One day of heavy spring rain and the smolts are gone. As the saying goes, "The first spate in May takes the smolts away." If there is any appreciable current, the smolts descend tail first so that water flows through their mouths and over their gills and thus provides them with oxygen. In slack water they turn and swim downstream. After an acclimation period in the estuaries, the smolts then proceed to the North Atlantic (Figure 1-2), particularly to the waters around Newfoundland (though there is some indication that *grilse*, salmon that return to the rivers after spending one year at sea, spend their winter relatively close to the mouth of their natal river). Tagging studies show that many European salmon migrate across the North Atlantic to join their American relatives (Figure 1-3). Icelandic salmon, however, seem to prefer an area off the Faroe Islands (located between Iceland and Scotland). There has been much speculation, but little scientific proof, as to how the salmon accomplish this feat of navigation, as well as their return to the rivers after several years at sea. There is no question, however, that they recognize their home river on the return trip by its distinctive odor.

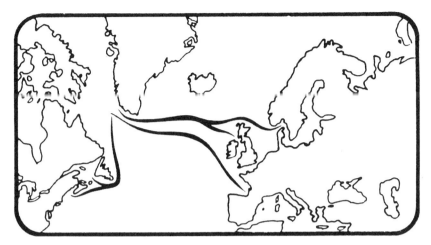

FIGURE 1-3. *Migration of European Atlantic salmon to the Labrador Sea feeding grounds.*

After a summer of feeding off Newfoundland, the fish move a bit south for the winter. During their second summer at sea they move northeast to the rich feeding grounds along the coasts of Labrador and western Greenland (the Labrador Sea). Typically the salmon start the long return trip to their native rivers during their second winter at sea, although some may remain in the ocean for a third, and a few even a fourth, year.

The salmon's diet at sea consists of a variety of creatures, including krill (a small shrimplike crustacean), capelin and rainbow smelt, alewives and other herrings, mackerel, sand lances, and small cod. The fertility of these waters allows the salmon to feed voraciously, which is reflected in its rapid growth. Hence, a fish that returns after 13 or 14 months in the ocean can weigh about 5 pounds (2.3 kilograms). A fish that has spent one year at sea is called a grilse, though it is otherwise indistinguishable from a two-sea-year fish, which returns weighing 8 to 12 pounds (3.6 to 5.4 kilograms), or from a fish that has spent three or four years in the salt, which can weigh 15 to 40 pounds (6.8 to 18.1 kilograms).

SPAWNING

The returning fish remain in the estuaries for some time, moving in and out of the brackish water to complete their adjustment to a freshwater environment.

Once acclimated, the first group of adult salmon starts upriver as the year's smolts are being washed out to sea. Early arrivals often make a dash for the head of the river, with a minimal number of resting stops. Later arrivals may take much of the summer to travel the same distance, with recuperation periods in deep water and in coldwater pools if river temperatures become too high. Such pools are fed by a brook or stream, which produces a tongue of cold water in which the salmon can survive until a change in weather cools the main stream to acceptable levels. In very warm weather, coldwater pools may be packed with fish.

Some rivers have only a summer run of salmon, others only a fall run; still others have both. This is one of nature's many safeguards to ensure that sufficient numbers of fish reach the spawning beds.

Having survived all hazards—the predators of parr and smolt, the hazards of the migration and the return to the rivers, the netters, the poachers, and the anglers—the salmon reach their spawning beds in late October.

The henfish selects a section of gravelly bottom having the correct contour, depth, flow, and gravel size (Figure 1-4). It must have a section of deeper water at both the upper and lower end. In an action known as *cutting*, the henfish, while lying on her side, bends her body in an arc, and then forcefully straightens it so that her tail acts as a shovel (Figure 1-5). (Researchers argue whether this is accomplished by contact of the fish's tail with the gravel or by water currents generated by the flapping tail.) The depth of the hole depends on the size of the female and, to some extent, on the speed of the current. An average two-sea-year hen will dig to a maximum depth of about a foot (30 centimeters). This excavated area is called a *redd*.

Closely attended by the cockfish, the female releases some of her eggs into

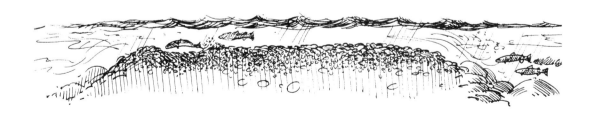

FIGURE 1-4. *A typical salmon spawning bed.*

the redd while the cockfish simultaneously releases some of his milt. The female then moves upstream and digs a second hole. The current carries the displaced gravel down to the first group of eggs and covers them. This process is repeated until all of the hen's eggs are deposited.

The male may be challenged during spawning by another cockfish, which evokes a stylized response. The dominant male faces the intruder and by erecting his fins, attempts to scare him into retreat. The male's *kype* (a hooklike projection of his lower jaw formed just prior to spawning) adds to his ferocious appearance. If this display fails, he dashes at his competitor with gill covers flared and mouth open. This usually causes the intruder to move off, though he may return a number of times before spawning is completed.

The female also has a stylized response to an intrusion by one of her sex. A henfish preparing to cut will take exception to the presence of another female located upstream of her. In response, she will swim up beside the intruder and slightly ahead of her. Her rival will then move to take the lead, after which this sequence repeats itself. Invariably, the intruding fish is forced away.

J.W. Jones (1959) describes his observations of spawning salmon in a tank constructed on the banks of the River Alwen, a tributary of the River Dee in Wales (not to be confused with the major salmon river of the same name in Scotland). The inshore walls of the 24 x 5½-foot (7.3 x 1.7 meter) structure (4 to 5 feet or 1.2 to 1.5 meters deep) contained thick glass observa-

continued on page 12

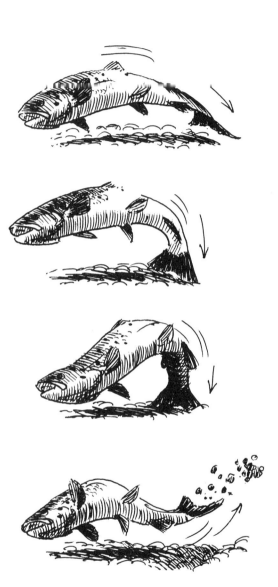

FIGURE 1-5. *Henfish digging a hole for the deposition of eggs. The cutting operation.*

SCALE READING

You can tell the salmon's life history by reading one of its scales—a process similar to reading the rings of a tree. This was discovered early in the twentieth century, and has become a standard procedure in salmon research. The following description was abstracted from an excellent article by Dr. Geoff Power, Professor of Biology at the University of Waterloo, Ontario, which appeared in the Winter 1987 issue of the *Atlantic Salmon Journal*. Dr. Power kindly supplied the photograph (Figure 1-6).

A salmon starts to develop scales at a length of 1½ inches (3.8 centimeters). The scales first appear in the fish's sides, near its tail, accumulating in parallel rows as it grows. Eventually the fish is covered with scales. Lost scales are replaced, giving the fish a fixed number of scales for life.

As the fish grows, the scales grow as well. Every few days the scales—which are made from a calcic, bonelike material—add a *circulus*, a concentric circle appearing as a slight ridge on the scale. The faster the fish grows, the farther apart are the circuli. In the fall, the fish's feeding rate decreases, and the circuli form closer together. As winter approaches they become indistinct and incomplete.

During the parr years they are not formed at all during the winter, but start to appear again in the spring when normal feeding commences. As soon as the fish reaches the sea it feeds heavily, and the circuli become widely spaced (with a proportional decrease during winter). In Figure 1-6, numbers 1 through 5 indicate the closely spaced circuli of slow winter growth during the fish's five years of parr life. The widely spaced circuli beyond number 5 correspond with the fish's first season feeding at sea. This is followed by a winter mark (due to reduced winter feeding) and, at A, a so-called spawning mark, caused by scale erosion during spawning as the fish draws on them to replenish its supply of calcium. If the salmon survives spawning, scale growth resumes as the kelt mends in the ocean, but the scale is scarred. The spawning marks at B and C show the fish was returning for a fourth spawning when this scale was taken.

A regenerated scale will not show events in the salmon's life before the previous scale was lost. According to Dr. Power, as many as 70 percent of a salmon's scales may be regenerated. Therefore, he advises you remove at least a dozen scales to be sure you get at least one original.

FIGURE 1-6. *Magnified scale of a salmon.*

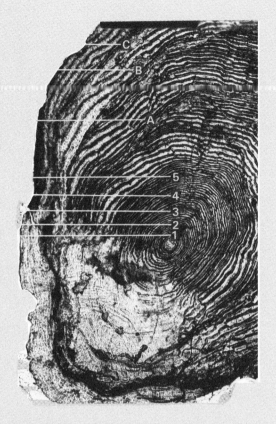

Remove a scale by first removing mucus from a small area between the dorsal and anal fins and just above the lateral line with a knife blade, scraping toward the tail. Then scrape the blade in the opposite direction to remove the scales. Clean the scales by then soaking them in detergent and allowing them to dry. You can store them in an envelope, on which you should record all pertinent data (date of capture, etc.).

Removing scales from a fish you intend to release introduces the possibility that bacteria may enter the scraped area. How serious this risk is no one can say for certain. But I'm of the opinion you should avoid *any* unnecessary risk to the fish.

tion windows. Gravel in which salmon had previously spawned was taken from other sections of the river and was spread on the river bed within the tank. Deeper areas were left at each end to simulate a natural redd. Jones found that if salmon in the enclosure were ready to spawn, nothing he did would deter them, including tapping on the glass or switching on powerful photography lights. (It is noteworthy, however, that the fish *were* disturbed if a shadow fell across the window from inside the observation area.) Using this tank, Jones was the first to observe the salmon's spawning behavior in detail.

The Parr as a Father

Male parr that have reached a proper size will ripen into sexual maturity during the summer and fall and move into the spawning areas along with the returning adults. (Female salmon never ripen until they return from the sea as mature fish.) Two or three male parr will join a pair of mature fish on the redds, and there will be some jockeying for position among them. The parr will remain in position when the female starts to cut, despite the shower of stones she generates. Resenting the presence of parr, both adults pursue them with open mouth, though they never actually harm them. By positioning himself below, and just behind the hen's vent, the male parr is out of sight, and will not be disturbed by the adults. When the female has completed cutting, the parr will retreat to the bottom of the bed. When a shower of eggs descends on him he will release his milt with an excellent chance of fertilizing the eggs. The male parr, in fact, has a much better chance of fertilizing the eggs than does the adult male, whose milt will be diluted and partially dispersed by the current.

Jones found that henfish would not spawn unless an adult male were present. This defeated his experiment to determine if the progenies of parr were equal in size and vigor to those fathered by an adult. To get his answer, Jones had to provide a castrated male. As it turned out, the progenies of parr were identical to those having adult fathers. Jones therefore proposed that ripe parr contribute significantly to spawning success—another example of nature's ensuring the species' survival.

Repeat Spawners

At the completion of spawning, which may take a week or more for some individuals, both partners are exhausted. The female seeks out a pool to rest, but the male stays on the redds to fight with other males and, if he is not completely spent, to spawn with other hens.[1, 2]

At this stage, Pacific salmons die automatically, triggered by a hormonal release. Many Atlantic salmon die as well, though some live to return to the ocean. If the river is short, they may be able to make it back before ice blocks their exit. Often this is not possible, as spawning may take place over 150 miles (240 kilometers) upstream. Hence, many salmon must attempt to endure in the rivers until spring—still without significant feeding.

The fish seek out a deep pool to escape the ravages of the winter ice. With the spring thaw the few survivors, now referred to as *kelts* or *black salmon*, descend to the ocean, where they feed voraciously. These fish will return to the river the following year for a second, and perhaps even further spawnings (some females have reportedly spawned as many as five times). Most repeat spawners are females, and although few in number they are very important. With their additional year of ocean feeding, their increased size will provide a larger number of eggs than are provided by first-time or *maiden* spawners. Consequently, repeat spawners make a greater individual contribution to the future stock of the river.

On New Brunswick's Miramichi River there has long been an organized sport fishery for kelts. Ravenous from their winter fast, they will take a large streamer fly without hesitation in the high waters of the spring runoff. Kelts must be released under the same rules that presently apply to adult *bright fish*; these must be returned to the river if they exceed 24.8 inches or 63 centimeters in length. It seems quite possible that battling an angler could significantly diminish a kelt's chances of reaching the sea alive. It is difficult to imagine that a fish that has suffered the rigors of spawning, spent the winter in a frozen river, and fasted for nearly a year would fare very well in a fight. However, some anglers claim that kelts feed heavily on parr during their descent, which would be a minus in terms of maintaining the stock. Because parr are produced in such large numbers, though, perhaps the loss of some of them would be outweighed by the advantage of sustaining repeat spawners.

Notes

1. Tagging records show that most repeat-spawning salmon are females. Perhaps the cockfish's dalliance on the redds reduces its chances of returning to the sea.

2. A cockfish I caught in Quebec's Matane River on August 16, 1966 had spent three years in the river as a parr and two years at sea before spawning. He then returned to the ocean for one year. I caught him on his second spawning run, at which time he weighed 14 pounds, 5 ounces (6.5 kilograms), and was 36½ inches (92.7 centimeters) long. This life history was obtained by reading one of the fish's scales—a process similar to reading the rings of a tree. The reading was done by Gilles Shooner, who at the time was the resident biologist on the Matane for the Quebec Wildlife Service. Gilles also showed me a scale reading from a salmon of 30-plus pounds (13.6-plus kilograms). The reading showed the fish had already spawned four times, and was returning for a fifth when caught. As far as Gilles knew, that was a record number of returns to the Matane at that time.

CHAPTER 2

Equipping for Salmon

In the Spey I enjoyed one of the best day's sport (perhaps the very best) I ever had in my life: it was in the beginning of September, in close time; the water was low, and as the net fishing had been given over some days, the lower part was full of fish. By a privilege, which I owe to the late Duke of Gordon, I fished at this forbidden time and hooked twelve or thirteen fish in one day. One was above 30 pounds and broke me by the derangement of my reel.

—Sir Humphrey Davy, *Salmonia*

Rods

Fly rods have evolved from 19-foot, several-pound lancewood, greenheart, or hickory monsters, through split bamboo, fiberglass, boron, and finally to present-day graphite. In the early seventeenth century, dry salmon flies were unknown. Wet flies were cast with a fixed length of line barely longer than the rod. In the twelfth century, the Chinese had invented the reel, but it had to be reinvented some 500 years later in Europe before it was available to the early salmon anglers. Even then the reel was not widely used until silk lines replaced those made of braided horsehair. Of necessity, horsehair lines were knotted every few feet. Although these knots were wound with silk thread, they could still catch in the guides (or *rod-rings*, as they were then called), thereby rendering a reel impractical.

A rod of at least 17 feet (5 meters) was needed to throw the large flies then used. With no reel, a short line, and a horsehair leader, those early anglers must have lost a high percentage of the salmon they hooked. There is some indication that the anglers, upon hooking a fish, threw the rod into the river, allowing the salmon to tow it about until it tired.

By 1900 the silk line came into general use. The lack of knots made reels more feasible, which led to shorter rods, most often made of the newly popular split bamboo. In the early 1900s, Edward R. Hewitt (1950) used a bamboo rod of 14 feet (4.3 meters), and weighing 16 to 18 ounces (450 to 510 grams), for his wet-fly salmon fishing. Hewitt dismissed the traditional rods then in use—17 feet (5.2 meters) in length and weighing 28 ounces (790 grams)—as being "very tiring to use" and "not necessary in our rivers . . . for clear water fishing, the most satisfactory all-around rod for the angler who casts well is the 5¾ ounce [163 grams], 10 foot [3 meters] tournament model, single-handed rod which weighs, with reel seat, 6 ¼ ounces [177 grams]." We should note that in this period Hewitt, along with George M.L. LaBranche and Ambrose Monell, was fishing for salmon with dry flies; so certainly a single-handed rod would be better than a two-hander to perform the necessary line recovery during the float.

The split-bamboo salmon rod remained unchallenged until the end of World War II and the introduction of fiberglass rods. Resin-impregnated glass cloth, wrapped around a mandrel and heated in a pressurized mold, produced a hollow rod that was substantially lighter than a bamboo rod of equivalent power. The quality of these early glass rods varied greatly, however. I recall in those years meeting a salmon angler on Quebec's Matane River who was casting a beautiful long line using a glass rod. He told me a friend of his turned them

FIGURE 2-1. *Nineteenth-century salmon anglers.*
(Courtesy of the American Museum of Fly Fishing, Manchester, Vermont)

out in large quantities to sell at a low price to bait-fishers. He said the quality was very erratic, but he could tell by flexing them as they came down the production line which blanks might be good. These he would test by casting. A few rods met his standards and were retained; the others he returned to his friend for the worm-dunking trade.

In a few years the manufacturing process improved considerably, and excellent glass rods became available. Relative to split bamboo, glass rods were less expensive to manufacture. This made it possible for persons of limited means to take up fly-fishing. Being lighter than bamboo rods of equivalent power, glass rods were of particular interest to salmon anglers who spent long days astream.

By the early 1970s, graphite began replacing fiberglass, using technology developed in the aircraft industry. Lighter and stronger than glass, graphite further reduced the rod's weight and increased line speed.

Weight is by no means the only consideration in choosing a rod. Aesthetically, nothing compares to split bamboo. For some anglers, this consideration outweighs all others. Even today, customized bamboo rods are a thriving, if limited, industry.

To begin salmon fishing, I recommend a 9-foot (2.8 meters) graphite rod for an 8- or 9-weight line. The choice between these two is largely determined by the size of the water you're fishing. Larger waters are more subject to strong winds, which the 9-weight line will handle better than will the 8-weight. Of course, most graphite rods can handle lines with adjacent weight numbers.

Long rods are sometimes furnished with detachable butts (less often on rods of 9 feet [2.8 meters] or less). A longer butt helps keep the reel clear of clothing during the play. A butt of about 2 inches (5 centimeters) long is sufficient. This is easily stored in a vest or wading jacket, and can be attached to the rod after the hookup. However, few salmon anglers, I find, ever use their detachable butts—either because they consider them a nuisance or because they simply forget. There seems to be a trend toward permanent short butts on salmon rods. In a long battle with a fish of 20 pounds (9.1 kilograms) or more, it can easily prevent your clothing from becoming entangled in your reel during the play—a pitfall that could cost you a fish.

Rod choice is ultimately a personal preference. Lee Wulff, who pioneered the use of short rods for Atlantic salmon, demonstrated that the long casts often required in salmon fishing could be accomplished with light fly tackle. He noted, however, that "rods of less than eight-and-a-half feet [2.6 meters] are for those with special qualifications both in casting and in playing of fish." He further noted that the maximum pressure you can exert on a 2-pound (0.9 kilogram) trout is the same for a 20-pound (9.1 kilograms) salmon. We should point out, however, that inadvertently exerting a pressure that will lose your fish (either by the tippet's breaking or the hook's pulling out) is much more likely with a salmon because of its greater acceleration. Reacting slowly to a salmon's sudden run can be disastrous.

Your fly rod's most important quality is that it suit your casting style. This can only be established by trial; rarely will lawn-casting behind the shop be sufficient. Some dealers will lend a demonstration rod to a customer for a day or

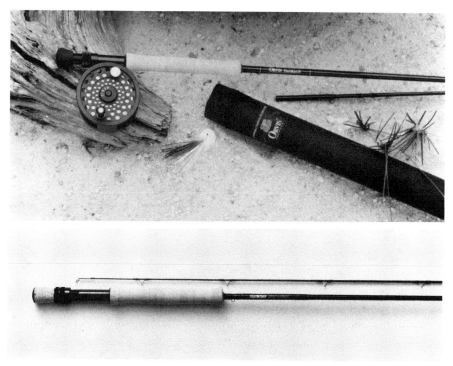

FIGURE 2-2. *Salmon Rods. Upper: Orvis Matrix Power-10 909. Bottom: Sage 990 RPL-X.* (Courtesy of Orvis, Sage)

so. Should you purchase a rod by mail order, find out beforehand the dealer's policy on returns.

My personal choices in salmon rods include the L.L. Bean Double L B710KH (made by Loomis), the Scott G908, and the Sage GFL 990 RPL-X (Figure 2-2, bottom). I have not fished with the Orvis Power Matrix-10 908 or 909 (9-foot [2.7 meters] rods for 8- and 9-weight lines, respectively), but I have cast the 909 (Figure 2-2, upper) extensively, and am convinced these rods represent a breakthrough by Orvis. The full Wells grip of these rods allows for a good power stroke with the thumb-on-top grasp—the only grasp to use with a rod of this size.

Another important consideration in choosing a rod is the size and shape of its grip. When trying out a rod, pay as much attention to how the handle fits your hand as you do to the rod's action. A handle too small or too large will be very tiring to use, and will detract from your casting. This is one reason you'll need more than a few dozen casts to evaluate a rod properly. A handle that is a bit too large, or that isn't exactly the right shape, can be improved by careful sanding. But a rod whose handle is too small will soon be gathering cobwebs in your rod rack.

Reels

Lighter graphite rods need lighter reels to balance them. Thus, frames made of machined lightweight aluminum alloys combined with ventilated spools have become ubiquitous.

Another development is the exposed-rim spool, a feature almost universal on single-action reels. Prior to this, you controlled the fish's run by jamming the running line against the rod butt with your forefinger, which gave variable braking and sometimes caused friction burns. Palming the exposed rim gives you excellent control over a running fish, minus the burns.

This is an appropriate time to comment on *antireverse reels.* When fishing, you select a drag setting on your reel that will not cause your leader to break if a salmon takes a sudden lunge during the play. With a direct-drive reel you know that every turn of the handle retrieves line, and that when the fish is running, you had better keep your hand away from the rapidly rotating handle. The handle of an antireverse reel does not rotate when a fish takes line. You can keep on mindlessly turning the handle even as the fish is moving away, instead of slowing his run with rim control. Even if you realized what was going on, you might not be able to palm the rim, because many antireverse reels do not have exposed rims. As a result, the fight will be prolonged, lessening the fish's chances of survival when you release it. Antireverse reels have no place in salmon fishing.

The ratio of diameter to width (D/W) in the spool of a salmon reel is an important consideration (Figure 2-3). If a hooked salmon runs directly at you, you must recover the slack as quickly as possible. Otherwise the fish will shake the hook and be lost. One solution is a *multiplier reel,* which gives greater than one spool revolution for each rotation of the handle. These reels are more complex mechanically than single-action reels and are therefore more expensive. In the past they have been prone to breakdown and for this reason had, until recently, almost disappeared from the market. At this writing, my experience with the newly introduced multipliers has been too brief to report on their reliability.

Another way to quicken line recovery is to use the maximum amount of

FIGURE 2-3. *Critical dimensions in a salmon reel spool. The ratio D/W should be at least 2.7 and preferably up around 3.0.*

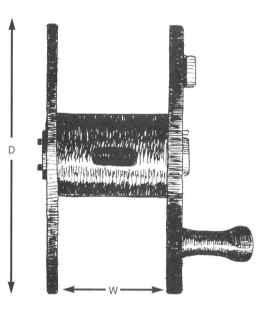

FIGURE 2-4. *My choice of reel for salmon fishing, below, is the Scientific Anglers System 2-M, either the Model 78 or the Model 8/9. The Model 78 holds a WF8F and 120 yards (109 meters) of 20-pound-test (9.1 kilograms) backing; the 8/9 holds a WF9F and 180 yards (164 meters) of the same. The Orvis Battenkill 8/9, right, will take a WF9F and 150 yards (137 meters) of backing.* (Courtesy of Scientific Anglers, Orvis)

backing (limited by the size of the reel) or by decreasing the spool width (W, Figure 2-3) so that the layer of backing on which the incoming line is being wound is greater in diameter. But to keep the capacity of the reel unchanged it will be necessary to simultaneously increase the spool diameter (D). The pertinent dimensions for a variety of reels are given in Table 2-1. The large Pflueger Medalist, one of a previous generation of salmon reels, had a D/W of 3.00. It was an excellent reel, but lacked an exposed rim to compete with the present-day instruments of salmon fishing. The Hardy Salmon 1, with a D/W of 3.18, is a longtime favorite of mine. System 2M reels (Figure 2-4), which are large enough to hold a salmon backing, have an even higher D/W. The Orvis Battenkill 8/9 (Figure 2-4) is quite a wide reel, which puts it on the D/W borderline, but it has a number of redeeming features to recommend it, such as smooth drag and light weight. The salmon reels with the lowest D/W's seem to be disappearing from the market, but take along a ruler when you go shopping for a reel.

TABLE 2-I

Dimensions of Fly-reel Spools (in sixteenths of an inch)

Reel	Diameter (D)	Width (W)	D/W
Battenkill (8/9)	54	20	2.70
System 1 (456)	47	12	3.92
System 1 (678)	47	16	2.94
System 2M (78)	53	13	4.08
System 2M (89)	53	16	3.31
Hardy Marquis Salmon 1	51	16	3.19
Pflueger Medalist	48	16	3.00

Your salmon reel must be large enough to hold your fly line plus a minimum of 100 yards (91.4 meters) of 20-pound-test (9.1 kilograms) braided-Dacron backing. (In most cases, a reel's backing capacity is specified for a weight-forward fly line, used almost universally in salmon fishing.) Backing requirements depend both on the size of the largest fish expected and on the amount of unobstructed water in which it can run. It pays to err on the high side, but having extra backing doesn't mean you should allow a fish to run farther than necessary (see Chapter 8). Remember that excessive backing, especially if you choose 30-pound test (13.6 kilograms), means that you will need a larger reel—more expensive and more tiring to use. You can increase the amount of backing a reel can hold by shortening the running end of your fly line. This will allow you to get by with a smaller, lighter, and less expensive reel.

Most reels can be converted to either a left-hand or right-hand retrieve. When I began fly-fishing, all reels were right-handed. Some anglers argue that you should use your dominant hand to hold the rod while playing the fish, leaving your weaker hand for the less demanding job of winding. I've never found this convincing, and to this day I both cast and wind with my right hand. It comes down to what's comfortable for you.

Most reels come equipped with a clicker, which is seldom possible to turn off. The click contributes negligibly to the reel's drag, and creates too much noise for my liking. I admit this is a minority opinion; most anglers delight in hearing the reel sing with a running fish. The reel's drag during casting should be adjusted so that the energy of the cast just suffices to pull a few inches of line off the spool.

LINES

Casts to salmon are most often 40 to 50 feet (12 to 15 meters), so weight-forward-taper fly lines are used most often. Capacity considerations rule out double-taper lines, but Lee Wulff's Triangle Taper lines are a viable alternative, especially if the rivers you fish require much roll casting. The heart of the salmon season in North America runs from early July to mid-September, corresponding with river temperatures between 50 and 70 degrees F (10 and 21 degrees C). Under these conditions, you'll need only a floating line. A possible exception is during a heavy flow, when a sink-tip line might be preferable. In the colder waters of June, the last two weeks of September, and throughout October, a sink-tip line will offer an advantage. The salmon season in Great Britain begins in February, when the water is just above freezing; then, fast-sinking lines and large flies are the norm (Ashley-Cooper, 1983).

The average cast in salmon fishing is a good deal longer than the average cast to trout. Long casts in themselves, however, offer no advantage to the salmon angler. In fact, they are often a disadvantage: Long casts are usually less accurate, and a long line stretches more than does a shorter line, reducing your ability to set the hook. On a large river, a long cast is sometimes necessary to reach a fish if wading closer is impossible. For this reason I favor a line such as Scientific Anglers' Steelhead Taper, because its "long-belly" taper makes for easier shooting.

Incidentally, if you feel your casting could stand improvement, I recommend the video *Fly Casting with Lefty Kreh*. By adopting Lefty's unique casting system, most anglers can increase their casting distance and greatly enhance their technique. The five principles of Lefty's casting system are:

1. The rod is a lever that moves through an arc whose length is directly related to the casting distance: short arcs for short casts, long arcs for long casts.
2. Before making a back cast you must have the line clear of the water and moving. Therefore, start with your rod tip close to the water's surface.
3. The line will go in the direction in which you accelerate and stop, both on forward casts and back casts.
4. There is a direct correlation between the length of the acceleration step and the loop size. Short acceleration and a quick stop give a tight loop and, consequently, a longer cast.
5. To make a long cast, or to deal with anything that makes casting difficult (such as headwinds or large or wind-resistant flies), you must follow principle number 1 and move the rod through the maximum arc (180 degrees). To do this you need to back-cast at 45 degrees to the surface, then cast forward with your forearm only and at 90 degrees—all with no wrist action.

These principles apply to any specialized cast. By dropping your rod tip about "one frog hair" at the end of the forward cast, you'll eliminate tailing loops and the so-called *wind knots*.

LEADERS

One of the historic debates in salmon fishing concerns leader length and tippet diameter. Edward R. Hewitt (1950) believed in long leaders, with tippets as fine as possible. John E. Hutton in his 1949 book *Trout and Salmon Fishing* stated the opposite. Hutton once landed his limit of eight salmon using a 30-inch (76 centimeters), 0.019-inch-diameter (0.5 millimeter) level gut leader. The evidence in support of Hewitt's and Hutton's positions shows that their views weren't all that far apart.

Hewitt wrote of fishing over a group of salmon lying on a bar in about 2 feet (0.6 meter) of water. Using a dry fly and a 12-foot (3.7 meters) gut leader tapering to 0.014 inch in diameter (0.4 millimeter), he rose about 20 fish in a row but failed to hook any, noting, "They all seemed to miss the fly." Hewitt then tied on an additional 4 feet (1.2 meters) of 0.010-inch-diameter (0.25 millimeter) gut and hooked seven fish in a row with only a few missed rises. He attributed this success to lower visibility of the tippet and to a better float of the dry fly.

Hutton ordinarily used a 6½-foot (2 meters) length of gut to allow for easy casting. Hutton's experiment, using 30 inches (76 centimeters) of 0.019-inch-diameter (0.5 millimeter) level gut, was to test his claim that leader length and tippet diameter were of no importance in salmon fishing. Two of the eight fish Hutton took exceeded 20 pounds (9.1 kilograms). He remarked, "Some were taken in quite shallow glides with a #4 fly, while others fell victims to a 1/0 Silver Gray."

Hewitt wrote that he never used a longer leader or a finer tippet than was necessary. It may be significant that the incidents he cited to support his ideas involved dry-fly fishing, whereas Hutton's experiment employed large wet flies.

In general, salmon dry flies should be used with finer tippets than are used with subsurface flies. Arguably this has more to do with keeping the fly floating than it does with the fish's leader-shyness. Gut leaders had to be of a relatively large diameter to provide sufficient strength (see Table 5-1). If Hewitt had had access to modern tippet materials, he would have had no trouble in going fine enough for a good dry-fly presentation without having to compromise tippet strength.

Lee Wulff (1983) advocated using the longest leader that could be cast well and the finest tippet that the fly, and one's playing skills, would tolerate. Sound advice.

With salmon leaders you need a heavy butt (0.026 to 0.028 inch or 0.66 to 0.71 millimeter) to turn over the large and bulky flies that are often fished. This rules out leaders designed for trout, which typically have 0.018- to 0.022-inch (0.46 to 0.56 millimeter) butts. Salmon leaders are sold under such designations as Salmon, Steelhead, or Big Game. A length of 9 feet (3.3 meters) is a popular one, with tippet strengths ranging from 6 to 15 pounds (2.7 to 6.8 kilograms). When the river temperature drops below 50 degrees F (10 degrees C), it's important to fish your fly at least a foot (30 centimeters) below the surface. This requires the use of a sink-tip line and a short (4-foot or 1.22-meter) leader.

Commercial leaders are almost always knotless—not entirely out of convenience. Every knot is a point of potential weakness. In a knotted trout leader the strength of the material is so great in relation to the strength of the fish that, except for the tippet, a failure is highly unlikely. Even a poorly tied blood knot should not cause problems. Not so with a big salmon. The knots must be perfectly tied. (I have sour recollections of good fish lost through failure of one of my leader blood knots.) For this reason I prefer tapered, knotless salmon leaders. The Orvis Big Game brand is a good one, and permits the use of their high-strength tippet material. The largest salmon I ever landed weighed 33 pounds (15 kilograms). I used a knotted leader having four blood knots and a 15-pound (6.8 kilograms) tippet. Orvis had tied the knots well, but I decided at that point never to buy another knotted salmon leader. No sense in pressing my luck.

For most rivers, where the largest salmon you might encounter would weigh about 14 pounds (6.4 kilograms), use a 10-pound-test (4.5 kilograms) tippet. For big-fish rivers like the Restigouche, the Moisie, or the Grand Cascapedia, you should use a 15-pound-test (6.8 kilograms) tippet.

Tippet size is somewhat limited by the size of the flies you are using. Obviously you can't thread a 15-pound-test (6.8 kilograms) tippet through the eye of a size-12 fly, or turn over a 2/0 fly very well with a 6-pound (2.7 kilograms) tippet. Fortunately, most of the fishing for large salmon is done during periods of high water, when large flies are indicated. One July morning on the Miramichi I rose a large fish that did not touch my fly. After a good number of presentations, using size-6 and -8 flies, which were ignored, I hooked the fish with a size-10 Undertaker, but lost it when the hook pulled out in the rapids below the pool. The 6-pound (2.7 kilograms) tippet held up throughout the battle, which lasted more than 20 minutes. I estimate the fish weighed at least 15 pounds (6.8 kilograms).

I believe tippet size does influence a salmon's decision to take a fly. It seems to me that many, if not all, last-minute refusals are the fish's reaction to the leader rather than the fly dressing. As a result, I fish with the lightest tippet that will hold the fish I can anticipate catching. If I do not know what size fish to expect, I have to depend on information from my guide or a local angler. Guides' recommendations are often on the heavy side, perhaps because they fear their clients will be more unhappy with a breakoff than a refusal.

Playing skill is perhaps the most important factor in deciding tippet size. A beginner may fail to react quickly enough to a salmon's sudden change of direction and a blistering run. This angler needs a stronger tippet than one who has landed a thousand or more fish. Lee Wulff landed many salmon of 30 or more pounds with a 4-pound-test (1.8 kilograms) tippet. Father Elmer Smith, the inventor of the Bomber fly, customarily fished with 4-pound-test. As he believed that the sport was in getting the salmon to take, rather than in landing the fish, Father Smith would break the fish off if he could not land it within five minutes. He told me this often proved difficult.

We must conclude that, as with so many other aspects of the sport, there are no hard and fast rules but only broad generalizations to guide our decisions.

Whatever leader you use, the tippet material should be identical. That is, use Maxima tippet material with a Maxima leader; use Scientific Anglers tippet material with a Scientific Anglers leader. Mismatched leader-tippet combinations can result in poor knot strength.

Duramax the new ultrastrong braided leader material from Climax, has received a lot of press recently. At this writing I have not tested it extensively in salmon fishing. Its high strength and abrasion resistance would certainly be welcome. It is a good deal more visible in water than nylon of the same diameter. In addition, being braided material, it opens up to a larger apparent diameter when immersed in water. The balance of these pluses and minuses is yet to be established.

GLASSES

Glasses should be worn at all times while salmon fishing to protect your eyes from a fly misdirected by wind. The large flies and stiff winds endemic to salmon fishing make this an even more important safety consideration than it is for trout fishing. Prescription lenses should be equipped with a good pair of polarized clip-on lenses (assuming you don't have prescription sunglasses) having high ultraviolet absorption. Not only is the river's surface glare harmful to your eyes, but it can keep you from seeing fish. Anglers not needing corrective lenses should protect their eyes either with polarized sunglasses, or with safety glasses on overcast days.

FLY BOXES

I find it convenient to divide my salmon flies into categories by box (or by the side of a box):

1. Wet flies, sizes 6 and 8.
2. Wet flies, sizes 10, 12, and low-water ties.
3. Wet flies, sizes 4 and larger, plus streamers and bucktails.
4. Dry flies and commotion flies.

I also have a box for experimental ties and another for what I call change-of-pace flies (odd or little-used flies to pique the interest of fish that fail to respond to more familiar patterns). It is unnecessary to carry all these boxes on any given day. For example, you won't need large flies during low water (when

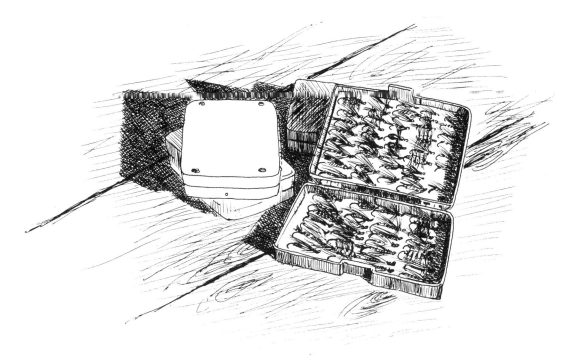

FIGURE 2-5. *At least one fly will appeal to today's salmon. See Chapter 7.*

boxes 2 and 4 would suffice); you probably won't need dry flies when the water temperature is below 50 degrees F (12.7 degrees C). I plan my day's fishing according to conditions (see Chapter 3), and put the flies I plan to use in a small auxiliary box.

OTHER EQUIPMENT

Fly flotant, hemostat pliers, a hook sharpener, and clippers should be on the checklist for any salmon-fishing vest. A stream thermometer is an essential piece of equipment (see Chapter 7). If you plan to keep a grilse for the table, be sure you carry a tag and a knife to slit the fish's tail (a single tag must be carried at all times to validate your salmon license, even if you do not plan to keep a grilse). A piece of light chain 24.8 inches long in your vest will tell if your fish is legal. In Canada, a grilse must be no longer than 63 centimeters or 24.8 inches. A mitt made from the foot of a woman's nylon stocking is handy for grasping the tail of

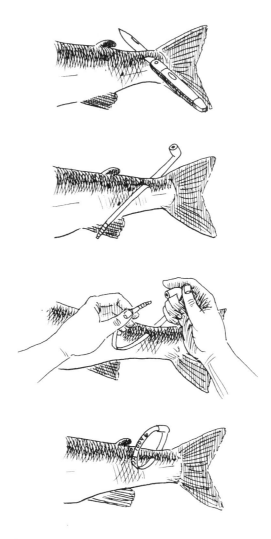

FIGURE 2-6. *Slitting the tail of a grilse to insert a tag.*
(Courtesy New Brunswick Fish & Wildlife)

a played-out fish, and also for holding a grilse while cleaning it.

Waders, vests, rain jackets, insect repellent[1], and wading staffs used for trout fishing will serve double duty on salmon rivers. Avoid brightly colored foul-weather gear on a salmon river (or a trout stream, for that matter); bright colors such as yellow will frighten the fish. Foul-weather gear should be a subdued green.

Putting it all Together

Let us now assemble our outfit. First we wind the fly line evenly onto the reel to find out how much space it occupies. If you are going to cut off some of the running line to increase your reel's backing capacity, now is the time to do it. Next, wind on enough backing to fill the spool to within about ¼ inch (about 0.6 centimeter) of the rim. Then wind the backing onto a parking spool while you remove the fly line. Pass the tag end of the backing around the reel arbor and around the standing part. Secure it with an *improved clinch knot*. Wind the backing evenly and tightly onto your spool. Take your fly line and strip a short length of the PVC coating from the running end using acetone or nail-polish remover. Join the length of exposed braid to the backing using a *simple blood knot* (see Figure 2-9). Now wind the fly line evenly onto the reel. It should fill the spool, leaving just enough room to rotate unimpeded.

Your line and leader are best joined with a loop-to-loop connection, which allows you to change leaders quickly and easily while on the water.

Most Orvis fly lines now come complete with a loop in their forward end. To whip a loop in the end of your fly line, double back the end to produce a loop about an inch (2.5 centimeters) long (A in Figure 2-7). Do not strip its coating. Put a spool of size-A thread (such as is used in rod wrapping) in your fly-tying bobbin. Pull about a foot (30 centimeters) of thread off the spool. Take four turns of thread around one arm of the bobbin before passing it through the tube. Trim the thread to at least 5 inches (about 13 centimeters) from the bobbin tip. Now grasp the two strands of line and the end of the thread with your left hand so that about ¼ inch (6.5 millimeters) of thread lies on top of the lines and extends toward loop A. Grasp loop A with your right hand, and then, using both hands in a circular motion, swing the bobbin so that the thread is wrapped tightly around the lines. The thread should sink into the coating of the fly line (if it doesn't, increase the speed of rotation and start the process over, but take more turns of the thread around the bobbin arm). Walk the rotating bobbin down toward the loop A. When you reach that point, cut off the bobbin, leaving a foot (30 centimeters) or more of standing thread. Take five more turns of thread around the lines and include the arms of a loop of 4X monofilament (C) in these windings. Now pass the thread through the monofilament loop D and pull on the ends of the monofilament. This will pull the tag of thread under the last five wraps. Give this thread a sharp pull to tighten these windings down on the underlying thread before trimming the end. Coat the completed wrappings with Pliobond, Aquaseal, or Goop.

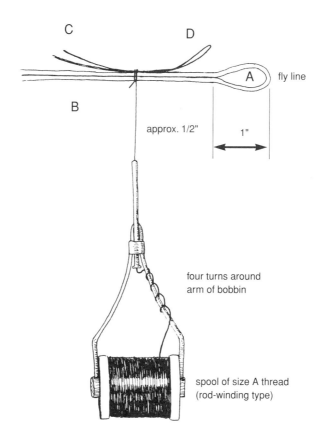

FIGURE 2-7. *Whipping a loop in the end of a*
fly line using Lefty Kreh's method.

The best way to put a loop in the butt end of your leader is with the *non-slip mono loop* (Figure 2-8).

The *blood knot* is widely used in all types of fly fishing, most often for building leaders. Properly tied, it is well suited for the job, but if constructed improperly it will be your downfall in landing a large salmon. The *simple blood knot* (Figure 2-9) is easier to tie, and is actually stronger than the regular blood knot. (For clarity, the two lines used are designated *black* and *white*.)

It is critical that you take exactly seven turns with each line. Start off with tag ends at least 6 inches (15.2 centimeters) long so that you will have a big circle to work with while making the second series of turns. Tighten the knot by

1. Tie a simple overhand knot forming loop 1 and pass the tag end back through loop 1 on the same side that it left. This forms loop 2 of the size desired in the finished knot.

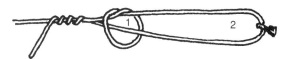

2. Make three turns of the tag end around the standing line.

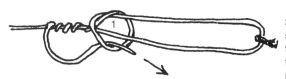

3. Pass the tag end through loop 1 on the same side that it left. Moisten the knot and tighten it by pulling on the tag end to tighten the wraps, then on the standing part and loop 2 simultaneously.

FIGURE 2-8. *Tying the non-slip mono loop knot.*

pulling alternately on the standing and tag ends. If you have tied the simple blood knot correctly, the tag ends will stand out at a 90-degree angle to the completed knot.

The other essential knot for the salmon angler is the *improved turle knot*, used to attach a fly to the leader. Although several other knots are a bit stronger (such as the improved clinch knot), the improved turle is preferred for salmon fishing because it pulls straight in line with the hook's shank, giving a more natural appearance to the swimming fly. With the salmon hook's turned-up eye, sporadic line tension would cause any fly attached with an improved clinch knot to lift its tail, destroying the illusion of a living thing. A straight pull along the shank also helps in hooking fish. Tying steps for the improved turle knot are illustrated in Figure 2-10.

It is essential to practice tying these knots so you can form them correctly and expediently on the water.

Now we will assemble the rod. Rubbing the male rod ferrule with a clear paraffin candle will prevent it from slipping during casting and jamming during disassembly. Disregard the oft-heard advice to lubricate the male ferrule with skin oil from your nose. This actually promotes slippage during casting and does a poor job of preventing jamming. You will be doing a lot of line shooting, mak-

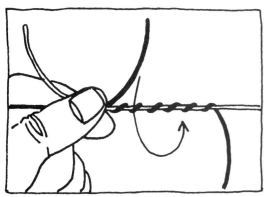

1. Cross the lines and hold the junction while taking seven turns with the black line around the standing part of the white line.

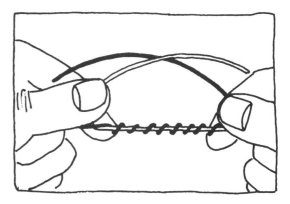

2. Pass the black line *behind* the white and grasp the cross-over point.

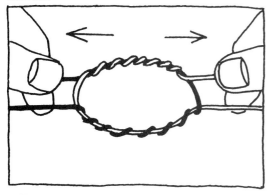

3. Take seven turns with the white line around the black.

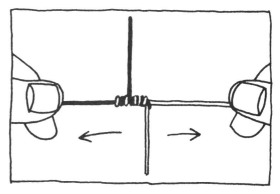

4. Moisten the knot and close the circle by pulling alternately on the tag ends and the standing lines.

FIGURE 2-9. *Tying the simple blood knot.*

ing it doubly important that your guides are lined up properly. When you sight down the assembled rod, the guides should be in a straight line from one side of the ferrule to the other.

Seat and lock the reel with care. The first salmon you hook could be a large one, and to have the reel come off your rod during the battle is an embarrassment you can do without. Thread the line through the guides, being careful not to miss any. It helps to double the leader back on the line and grasp the interlocked loops. Now put a bend in the rod by pulling the tippet while holding the reel handle. You will know immediately if you have missed any guides.

1. Pass the tippet through the eye and tighten an overhand knot in its end.

2. Tie a double overhand knot around the standing part of the tippet.

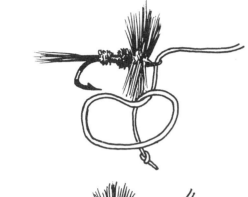

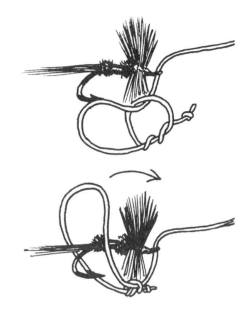

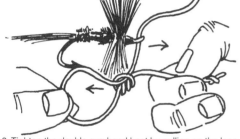

3. Tighten the double overhand knot by pulling on the loop and the tag end. Allow the single overhand knot to slide up against the main knot.

4. Pass the loop over the fly.

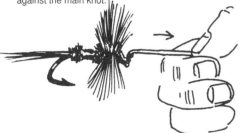

5. Wet the knot and tighten it, while preventing any hackle from being tied down in the process by holding it back with the hand that grips the hook.

6. Be sure the knot is pulled tight before trimming the tag end.

FIGURE 2-10. *Tying the improved turle knot.*

Maximum Pressure

To test the strength of your tippet, string your rod and tie on a fly. Hook the fly into a tree or fence post, then gradually put a bend in the rod as if to break the tippet. Almost surely the tippet will not break. Note the rod's arc when you feel you are applying maximum pressure. Consider this the limit for playing a fish. In practice, reduce this pressure by about 10 percent, for if a fish bolts suddenly as you are applying maximum pressure, it can easily break off. If you do break off a fish, chances are it will be at one of the knots: either at the knot joining the tippet to the leader or at the knot attaching the fly to the tippet. Knots are the weakest links in your terminal tackle, and you should take care to tie them correctly.

We can make this test more meaningful by suspending the leader from a hook and tying a pail to the tippet so that its bottom is just above the floor. Slowly add water or sand to the pail until the leader breaks. Now weigh the pail.

CARE AND MAINTENANCE

The size and vigor of salmon mean your equipment must be in top condition at all times. It makes no sense to make the proverbial thousand casts to hook a fish only to lose it because of equipment failure. The most common error is fishing with a fly whose hook point you've mashed on a rock during a back cast. A good guide will watch your casts, and will warn you to examine your fly if he sees a cast that is suspiciously low. A better solution is to develop a high back cast—but not even this is an absolute guarantee when there are tall rocks behind you.

So-called wind knots in your leader will greatly reduce its strength and can easily cause it to break while playing an active fish. These knots are often caused by a casting error known as the *tailing loop*, which occurs when the line coming forward on the forward cast contacts the line near the rod tip. It is easily corrected by dropping the tip of the rod a trifle just after you complete the power stroke. Don't overdo it; too extensive a drop will cause the line to be driven into the water rather than floating down to it softly. Remember that a very slight drop at the rod handle will cause a much larger drop of the tip some 9 feet (2.7 meters) away. This is fully covered in Lefty Kreh's casting video.

Inspect your leader without fail each time you complete coverage of a pool. Replace the leader whenever any hang-ups occur while playing a fish. Because the knot at the fly is a high-stress point in your terminal tackle, always retie the fly to the leader after releasing a fish.

Due to the accumulation of plankton and algae, your fly line will become dirty and sticky after about eight hours of fishing, so you should clean and dress your line before starting the next day's fishing. A clean fly line facilitates casting and is easier to handle. Stretch the line between two trees and clean it with one of the commercial preparations. By far the most efficient line cleaner is Armorall (the cleaner, not the polish). It is also the most economical. Since it was formulated for use on auto parts made of PVC, the same material used to coat fly lines, there is no danger of its being harmful. As you clean your line, inspect the leader for nicks and wind knots, and be sure that the interlocking loops connecting line and leader are in good shape.

Abraded Leaders and Other Hazards

Abrade a small section of the tippet with a rough stone, as might happen naturally while fighting a fish. Now apply tension as described in the above section on "Maximum Pressure." This will give you a clear idea of the disastrous effect a small abrasion can have on leader strength.

Nearly every knot reduces the strength of monofilament.[2] The worst is a simple overhand knot, which can reduce its strength by as much as 50 percent. You can confirm this easily with the pail-and-sand test. Exposing monofilament to sunlight or fluorescent light initiates a chemical reaction, which over time will also weaken it. Whenever measuring the strength of monofilament, soak it in water for at least 24 hours prior to testing. Nylon absorbs water, which in itself weakens it slightly. But as anglers, we are interested *only* in how it performs while wet.

You should conclude from this that you had better inspect your leader periodically for abrasions and wind knots, and make certain all the knots in your terminal tackle are tied properly.

Again, inspect your fly's hook point periodically. How often depends on the height of your back cast and the rockiness of the area behind you. Suffice it to say it is more than a little frustrating to miss a fish because of a dulled or broken hook point.

Many anglers have had their reels fall off while playing fish. When this happens there's a good chance you'll lose the fish or, worse, damage the reel. Make sure you bring the reel seat's locking nut up tight, and check it occasionally.

End-of-Season Maintenance

At season's end, examine the fly line for cracks in the coating. These are easily seen in light-colored lines because they fill with dirt, appearing as black lines. Cracks will appear first in the weight-forward section, because this is where the line flexes most during casting. If these cracks are deep enough, water will penetrate the nylon core and the line won't float properly. If the line is still serviceable, remove it from the reel, coil it over your forearm, secure the coils with pipe cleaners, and store it in a cool, dark place.

After removing the backing from the reel, clean the reel using warm soapy water and a toothbrush, rinsing it well. Dry the reel thoroughly with a hair dryer and lightly oil the spindle. The reel should then be ready for the following season. No care is required during the season other than an occasional drop of oil on the spindle and storage in a reel bag to keep out dust. Of course, should you get any silt or grime into the mechanism while fishing, wash the reel at once to prevent serious damage.

Notes

1. It has become common knowledge that Skin So Soft bath oil, distributed by Avon Products, has insect-repellent qualities. Unlike many commercial repellents, this product's water base does not harm the fly line's PVC coating. You can strengthen Skin So Soft by mixing it with full-strength DEET (N,N-diethyl-m-toluamide) in these proportions: 25 percent DEET, 25 percent Skin So Soft, and 50 percent water. Shake the container before applying. This mixture does a far better job repelling no-see-ums (also called *punkies*) than any commercial repellent I have tried.

2. There are a few knots that give nearly 100 percent strength: the *improved clinch*, the *Palomar*, the *Jansik special*, and the *surgeon's knot.*

CHAPTER 3

Understanding River Conditions

*Well, is your tackle all ready? It is a fine fresh
and cloudy morning, with a gentle breeze—a
day made for salmon fishing.*

—Sir Humphrey Davy, *Salmonia*

A SALMON RIVER IS AN INCONSTANT CREATURE. EACH DAY IT is different—most obviously in its height, more subtly in its temperature. It changes with the strength of the sun and the amount of upstream rain. Events in a major tributary can cause changes to a river that cannot be anticipated by anglers far downstream. These changes significantly affect how the salmon react to artificials.

During the early stages of the fish's upstream migration, both flow and temperature usually are to its liking. But the journey may take as long as five months, during which time the river's temperature and water level may fluctuate greatly. While five months may seem plenty of time for a fish to negotiate even the longest river, there are many obstacles it must overcome. There are rapids it must ascend, after which it must rest—both of which slow progress. If there are falls, they may require a certain flow before they can be jumped. This can mean more delays. A summer storm can turn the river into a torrent, which will hinder progress for several days (although it will facilitate progress after the extreme flow has abated). Drought coupled with hot weather can send water temperatures shooting to intolerable levels. During such periods the salmon must find cool water to hold in until a change in conditions allows them to continue upstream. (Salmon in rivers that have lakes for headwaters have an advantage here because of their river's more stable flow.)

Extremes in Flow

The salmon's movement upstream is called *running*. Salmon are most likely to take a fly just as they are about to run, or just after they have stopped running. Under normal water conditions and clear skies, the salmon's running occurs mostly at night. During its long upriver journey, however, salmon must contend with extremes in flow. These extremes greatly affect their running, and thus greatly affect the quality of angling.

Low Water

During a midsummer drought, when the pools are at their lowest and are connected by little more than trickles, salmon movement is difficult if not impossible. I have seen fish with their backs out of water, thrashing tails only partially submerged. Salmon survive these difficult times by holding up in pools that are cooled by tributaries or underground springs. Hundreds of fish will pack into these coldwater plumes, and will remain there until the rains come. In

text continues on page 44

CHANGING LIES

Figures 3-1 and 3-2 show a cross-sectional view of a river in high and normal flow. In normal flow, the site is unattractive to salmon. The limited depth here and at similar sites upstream has led the water to warm up, which in turn has deprived it of substantial amounts of dissolved oxygen—which has not been replaced by turbulence.

But a thunderstorm upstream brings the river up three or four feet, producing the situation shown in the upper illustration. Now the lies (positions outside the heavy current where salmon can rest) in the central flow, which were occupied before the storm, suffer from the increased flow. The salmon cannot afford to swim hard enough to maintain its position over them and retreats to the inshore position, which now provides water at a satisfactory temperature and a break in the current behind the large rock.

Spates

With luck, the rain will be just enough to return the river to its normal height and temperature. However, droughts are often broken by a *series* of rainstorms, creating a torrent. Water level ultimately depends on the amount of rainfall on the entire watershed. On a long river, it is possible to experience a sudden rise in water without any rain having fallen in your area.

The river's rise can be dramatic. Within a few days, a low-water river can turn into a debris-filled spate. Bog-fed tributaries will stain the river red. This is bad news for the angler, for the fish will hardly strike at all when the river is tainted. After such a spate, the river will run reddish for a week or more—disastrous for the angler with only a week's stay.

After a spate, fishing will not improve until the water level recedes and the water begins to clear. Fishing will then be poor to fair, but will improve as the water recedes further. You can fish at this stage with your largest wet flies (sizes 2 through 2/0). There is no point in casting out into the strong current, however. Any running fish will be close to the bank, or resting in an eddy. As the water level drops, decrease the size of your flies until you are back to size 6 and 8 at normal water level. It is during the latter stages of the drop, when the river is again running clear, that you'll have your best

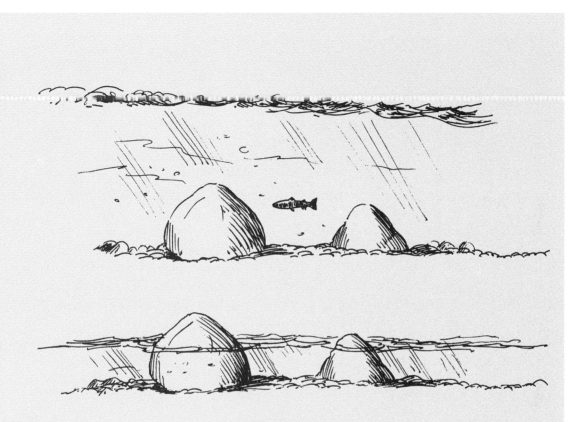

FIGURES 3-1 AND 3-2. *High flow (top) and normal flow (bottom).*

fishing. If you can time your trip to coincide with this, you'll be off to an excellent start.

As the water level drops and the river begins to clear, conditions will be more conducive to running, and the fish will begin to take. As the pools reach more moderate levels, the salmon will settle into their lies. We can now expect a period of good fishing. Water level is as close to normal as it will ever be. If you are lucky enough to have a series of moderate rains to maintain this favorable flow, and cool nights to keep the water temperature down, good fishing will continue.

A LIE'S DESTRUCTION

Salmon do not like to lie in turbulent water. Figure 3-3 shows a salmon lying on the very edge of the block flow around a rock (B), producing a lie that will often be occupied by a salmon when a run is in progress. During a spring runoff, however, the small submerged rock A is rolled by the high water into the critical position shown in Figure 3-4, an intrusion that creates turbulence as the two currents interact.

The fish now avoid a lie that has long been a hot spot for those who have fished the river, some of them for a good part of their lifetime, and they'll find it difficult to believe that this steady producer of taking fish has gone sour. Only when they find that other good lies are fishing as well as ever, will they have to admit that the problem is peculiar to this particular location.

If rock A is much lighter in color than the rest of the bottom rock in the vicinity, a knowledgeable angler might diagnose the problem. More often this is not the case and gradually the local anglers decide that this location is not worth exploring during their coverage of the pool. This could be a mistake, since another spring runoff may eventually move rock A downstream and restore the lie to its traditional importance. To a degree we fish a new river at the start of every season.

Rock A is not necessarily large, and most often the turbulence it produces is barely perceptible. The same situation can occur when a ridge of gravel is brought in by the current. I can recall one lie that stopped producing for unknown reasons until one day, while fishing a large double, I got the hooks fouled in what turned out

dead-low water, fishing is nearly impossible except in such pools. But despite their concentration, salmon are difficult to catch under these conditions. Your best chance is to cast to a solitary fish that has strayed from the crowd.

The drought eventually will be broken by thunderstorms. If these occur upstream, the fish will become agitated before there is any noticeable change in water level. They will mill about the pools with little inclination to take a fly. As the drought breaks and the river starts to rise, fish will gradually begin to move upstream, and fishing will improve. If you have been fishing size-8 and 10 wet flies, you can continue with these flies, moving to size 6s as the flow

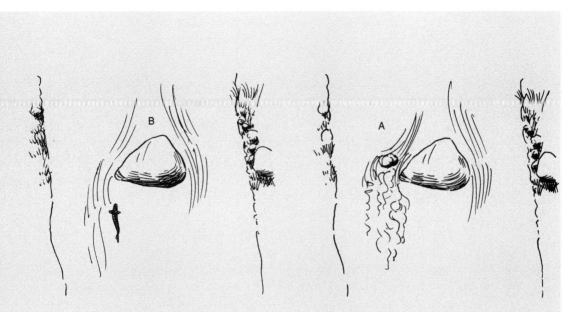

FIGURES 3-3 AND 3-4. *An established lie (left) can be rendered unproductive by turbulence caused by a small rock.*

to be a tree limb that had become jammed subsurface about the base of the key rock. In recovering the fly it was also possible to remove the limb. A few days later we took the first fish of the season off that lie, which remained productive for years until the key rock was moved downstream by heavy ice.

strengthens. A dry fly might be a better choice, however, especially if the water temperature is above 65 degrees F (18 degrees C). In general, wet flies are fished at normal to high water levels and cool to normal water temperatures (below 70 degrees F [21 degrees C]), while dry flies work better at lower water levels and higher water temperatures. You'll notice a 5-degree F (3-degree C) overlap when you can use either wet or dry flies. This rule is not fixed. There are a number of other conditions you might factor into your fishing strategy. I'll elaborate on these in subsequent chapters.

THE DAILY RIVER TEMPERATURE CYCLE

On an average summer day, with normal water level and bright sunshine, a river's temperature may rise 5 to 10 degrees F (2.7 to 5.5 degrees C). Overnight, most if not all of the temperature gained will be lost to radiation. An overcast during the day will eliminate or significantly reduce the river's warming. With high water, a river's temperature will hardly rise at all. Shading, both on the main stream and on the tributaries, is also important in moderating water temperature. In this regard, clear-cutting in a river's watershed is harmful; unfortunately, it is happening more often.

Water height and temperature should figure prominently in your salmon-fishing strategy. You should always carry a thermometer and read the river temperature a minimum of twice a day: first before you start fishing in the morning, and again when the sun is off the water in the evening. You can best measure changes in water level with a permanent gauge. To make one, select a solidly entrenched rock that has a smooth surface facing inshore. Paint lines on the smooth surface 2 inches (5 centimeters) apart and label the lowest *0* (dead-low water level) and the highest *8* (water too high for fishing). You may have to repaint the lines occasionally due to erosion. Lacking such a gauge, you can estimate water level from partially submerged rocks.

River height and temperature should help you decide which fly should begin your day's fishing. The last fly used the previous day should not automatically be your first fly simply because it is already on the tippet. As an extreme example, suppose it is autumn and that the preceding day had been extraordinarily warm, resulting in water temperatures in the low 60s F (16 to 17 degrees C). This, together with a normal flow, had persuaded you to fish with size-8 and -10 flies the previous evening. Overnight, radiative cooling and a drop in air temperature has sent the water temperature into the low 50s F (10 to 12 degrees C). This means you should use a size-4 or larger fly the next morning. If the overnight drop in temperature is only a few degrees, but a rain has caused the river to rise an inch or so, you should change to a larger fly as well.

RUNNING FISH

As we've said, under normal summertime water conditions most of the salmon's running occurs at night. However, on overcast days, and with a good flow of water, salmon will move almost continuously, with only a few minutes' rest after negotiating rapids or jumping falls. I once caught a tagged salmon on the

Miramichi that had moved upstream an average rate of 7 miles (11.2 kilometers) per day. From observations of identifiable fish (by way of scars or other deformities) we know they may stay on a particular lie from one day to a week or more. In some large, deep pools, such as those occurring where a major tributary enters, they may stay much longer. We will have much more information about the salmon's upstream movements when studies now underway are completed.[1]

If the fish are running at night, it follows that fishing will be best in the early morning (running just finishing) and at dusk (running about to commence). This would leave early afternoon as the worst possible time to fish—and this is what we experience, at least on bright days in July and August. On overcast days, or at water levels high enough to cause continuous running, time of day has no great influence on fishing success. In September and October, early morning offers the poorest fishing due to low overnight water temperatures and because the air is cooler than the water. The best fishing then is in the afternoon. Evening fishing can also be good during the fall, since the water temperature is near maximum then and the sun is off the water.

From reading the foregoing, you might conclude that the type and size of fly you use is governed strictly by water height and temperature. This assumes the salmon's behavior is consistent—which is not the case at all. If what you are using is not working, obviously you should make a change in your fly. But I would argue it might be better to first change the *size* of the fly you've been using, for I believe salmon react much more strongly to a fly's size than to its pattern. Whatever fly you choose, it should be one in which you have confidence.

Notes

1. At the mouth of the river, a miniature radio transmitter is placed in the fish's abdominal cavity and its upstream migration is monitored by radio.

CHAPTER 4

Wet Flies

The Traditional Cast

The Angle to the Flow

The traditional wet-fly cast is made quartering downstream. The angle to the current is typically 45 degrees, but it may be as much as 90 degrees or as little as 10 degrees, depending on water speed. Line and leader should immediately be tight. Slack will cause the fly to swim poorly, and will detract from your setting the hook.

The Wader's Casting Pattern

A casting pattern that gives you complete coverage of a pool is shown in Figure 4-1. Take position A, high enough upstream that cast number 1 will traverse the highest portion of the pool. Let the fly swing in the current until it dangles directly downstream. Before picking up for the next cast, give the line several hand retrieves. A fish will sometimes follow a fly into the dangle and will take it if it starts to move. The resulting hookup can be poor, but it's better

FIGURE 4-1. *Casting positions of a wading angler.*

than no hookup at all. Without moving, pick up and cast to position 2, and then to position 3. In each case, your fly should follow an arc identical to that of the first cast. Now take a step forward and repeat the procedure with casts to positions 4, 5, and 6. Working your way thus to the tail of the pool insures that any fish in the pool has a good chance of seeing your fly. You can cover a pool smaller than the one illustrated with fewer casts; for a larger pool, you'll need to make more casts. Depending on how intensively you want to cover a piece of water, you can vary the distance you step downstream between casts. For a very large pool you should fish the lies intensively, giving less coverage to the areas in between.

Some anglers wiggle their rod tip during the fly's swing, supposedly to give it a more lifelike appearance, though I've yet to see any demonstration that this is more effective.

Fly Speed

We do not know with any certainty why a salmon takes a fly. We do know, however, that the fly's speed is important in eliciting a strike. Knowing what constitutes ideal fly speed comes with experience. I know of no measurements, but I would estimate.it to be about 1½ to 2 miles (2.4 to 3.2 kilometers) per hour. The easiest way to attain ideal fly speed is to fish only those currents that are moving at that speed. This approach is far too wasteful, however. If your fly is moving too slowly, strip in line during the fly's swim. If your fly is moving too fast, decrease the angle of your cast to the flow. By casting a long line at a 10- or 20-degree angle to the current, you get a very short, but reasonably slow swim, even in rapidly moving water. You can use this technique to entice a salmon whose position you are reasonably sure of. Its drawbacks are that it gives the salmon only a brief, rear view of the fly, but this is sometimes enough to get the salmon to take.

GREASED-LINE METHOD

In the early 1900s Arthur H.E. Wood, fishing on Scotland's River Dee, developed a distinctive approach to wet-fly presentation he called *greased line fishing*.

In essence, greased-line fishing allows your fly to move close to the surface while maintaining a uniform speed for much of its swim, even when casting across stretches of unevenly flowing water. It also gives the fish a good broadside view of your fly.

How It's Done

Wood typically cast squarely across the current. If the water between you and your fly is flowing uniformly, you can allow your line to swing in a typical wet-fly arc. Since line and leader are moving downstream at the same speed as the fly, they do not affect its cross-current speed. If, however, you cast across fast water into slack (see position 1 in Figure 4-2), the current will bow the fly line downstream (position 2), pulling the fly quickly across the slack water. To counter the effect of the fast water, Wood threw an upstream mend into the line. Immediately after casting, hold the rod parallel to the water and lift the line free of the surface, swinging it gently upriver and a bit forward, depositing it in

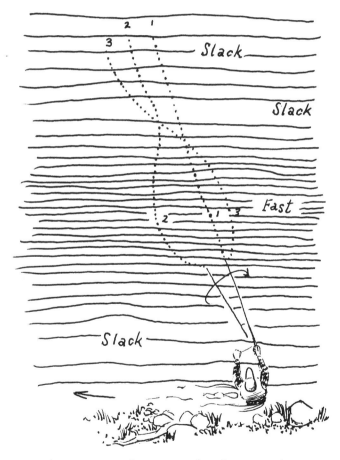

FIGURE 4-2. *Mending to remove downstream drag (Scott 1982).*

an upstream arc (position 3 of Figure 4-2). Done properly, the mend will not move the fly, and will delay the fly's cross-current acceleration until the fast water bows the line. When this happens, mend the line once more. To ensure that your mend gives no added motion to the fly, create a bit of slack by wiggling the rod tip before swinging the line upstream. The line mend is not a cast; it is a maneuver that puts an upstream bow in the line. Mending becomes more difficult as the line's downstream bow increases. It is easier to make two small mends than one large one. If you are casting across slack water into fast, mend downstream. Continuous mending requires that your fly line float at all times. The only way to make the silk lines of Wood's day float was to grease them—hence the name.

When to Use It

Wood briefly described greased-line fishing in Eric Taverner's 1948 book *Salmon Fishing*. He considered doing a book of his own on the subject, and discussed it with his friend "Jock Scott" (Donald G.H. Rudd), but died before he could complete the project. Scott had access to Wood's papers and had seen the outline of his book. These were the sources of his own *Greased Line Fishing for Salmon*. Due to the interest among steelhead fishermen in greased-line techniques, Frank Amato Publications came out with a new edition of the book in 1982.

Scott's book details a variety of fishing situations of importance to salmon anglers, such as the one illustrated in Figure 4-3. The main current entering the pool is split by a large rock at the head, creating a stretch of slack water between two fast sections. Imagine you are attempting to present a fly to the slack water at the far edge of the farthest stretch of fast water. Unless you mend the cast (1) promptly, the fly will be dragged out of the slack water and whipped across the far current (2). By the time your line reaches position 2 it is too late to mend. You can maintain position 3 for a time with continued mending. After your fly reaches 4, allow it to swing across the near current.

Keep your rod tip pointed at the fly at all times. If a fish moves to your fly, its dorsal fin will often cut the water. Do not set the hook as soon as the salmon takes the fly, Wood cautions. Rather, give it some slack, either by lowering the rod tip or by feeding line through the guides. This allows the current to pull the fly into the corner of the fish's mouth—an excellent hooking location (this tension may even be enough to set the hook). The line either will hold in the current, or it will start moving upstream with the fish. At this point, sweep the rod downstream to complete setting the hook. This method assumes we are fish-

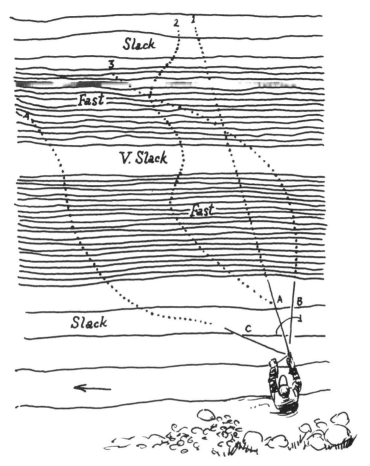

FIGURE 4-3. *Mending over two fast runs.*

ing with the small flies (sizes 6 through 10) commonly used over bright North American fish during the heart of the season. Wood believed these small flies would not be spat out by the salmon. Flies size 4 and larger are more liable to be rejected; therefore, sweep sooner to set the hook when using larger flies.

Wood's methods were widely adopted by British salmon anglers, particularly after Scott's book appeared. In his *New Angles on Salmon Fishing*, Philip Green writes of his initial enthusiasm for greased-line fishing and his subsequent realization that it needs to be restricted to specific situations. After a time, Green gave up casting squarely across the current. He also found that mending line could actually put off an interested salmon if it were done at the wrong time. Experience demonstrates that when a fly is cast downstream at a 45-degree angle and allowed to swing directly below the angler, a salmon is most likely to strike during the latter third of the swing. This final third is termed the *taking arc.* Green found that if he mended line while the fly was in the taking arc, interested fish often would turn off the fly. Green confines mending only to where water conditions make it necessary.

There are two occasions when I am inclined to use the greased-line method. The first is illustrated in Figures 4-2 and 4-3. The other is when I want to give an uninterested fish a different view of the fly (though I usually use a slack-line cast for this).

THE PATENT

As with all things pertaining to salmon fishing, it doesn't pay to be too rigid in your approach to wet-fly presentation. One time as I was fishing a pool of Quebec's Matane River, a fish showed on the bank opposite me above a lie defined by a submerged ledge. The bank was wooded to the water's edge. A wet fly was out of the question, because the fly would have been too far away from the fish window during most of its swim. A dry fly seemed my only option, but after wading as deeply as possible, I realized the lie was still too far away for me to present the fly effectively with the bamboo rod I then used. Finally convinced the fish was beyond my reach, I prepared to move, when the fish porpoised again, indicating it was likely in a taking mood. Extraordinary measures were justified. There is a presentation called *the Patent,* whereby you allow a hairwing fly to drift through a lie on a slack line. The rationale is that in the absence of cross-current fly movement, the undulating hairwing stimulates a take. Proceeding downstream, I waded across the river and made my way to just below the lie (the shoreline brush was too thick to move above the fish without spooking it). After replacing the dry fly with a size-8 Cosseboom wet, I rollcast upstream of the lie. I watched the fly's bright-yellow hackle as it tumbled down the current toward the fish's location. The salmon came up, rolling on its side with its mouth open. At first it seemed the fish was going to let the fly pass. But then, at the last possible moment, it took. I set the hook and moved out into the river to get the fish downstream into better water. It countered by bolting out of the pool and down a boulder-studded rapid. In hot pursuit, I threw line over the tops of the rocks. The fish was hooked well, and was still on the line when I got to the end of the rapid, where I landed it without further incident. If ever I truly earned a fish, it was that one.

But what about the dictum to always keep a tight line during the swim? Since this was the only time I have ever used the Patent, it would be inappropriate for me to comment further. However, the incident underscores the assertion that "never" and "always" are two words we should drop from our salmon-fishing vocabulary.

THE SLACK-LINE CAST

There are two critical aspects to presenting a fly to a fish: the fly's speed and its orientation to the current. Salmon may be put off by a fly traveling too fast, possibly because they are not in a mood to chase it, or perhaps because it seems unnatural. If we allow the current to control our fly's speed, it will more often than not be traveling too fast because of the cross-current acceleration. As we've already seen, mending may solve the problem. Another approach is the *slack-line cast*. To do this, cast 90 degrees to the current so that the fly lands upstream of

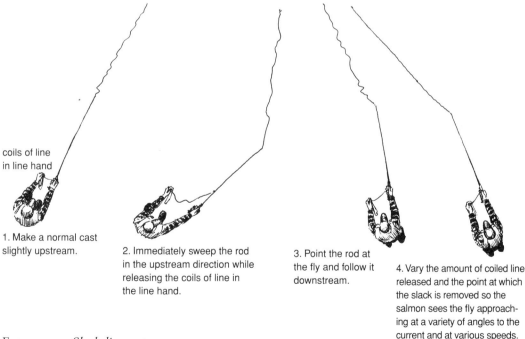

coils of line
in line hand

1. Make a normal cast slightly upstream.

2. Immediately sweep the rod in the upstream direction while releasing the coils of line in the line hand.

3. Point the rod at the fly and follow it downstream.

4. Vary the amount of coiled line released and the point at which the slack is removed so the salmon sees the fly approaching at a variety of angles to the current and at various speeds.

FIGURE 4-4. *Slack-line cast.*

the lie. As soon as the fly hits the water, hold the rod tip high and swing it upstream while releasing slack that you have coiled in your line hand. Immediately point your rod tip at the fly and follow it downstream as you gradually lower your rod tip. The slack will be taken up as the fly moves down the current, but the fly will not move across the current toward the fish until you remove the remaining slack. By varying the length of your casts, and by removing the slack at various distances from the lie, the fly approaches the salmon at a variety of angles and speeds. This approach generally will be more successful in getting a lethargic fish to take than will the traditional approach of changing fly patterns. The trout angler will recognize this cast as one often used to allow a nymph to sink before it approaches a feeding fish.

Why not mend line upstream here to prevent drag? Mending will certainly do this, but it will not allow for the variety of fly approaches that the slack-line cast does. Mending is for when you need to search for a taking fish, in which case you need to minimize fly acceleration over the full range of the swim. After locating a fish, the slack-line method allows you to discern just the right direction of approach and speed your fly should have.

LIES

As you become familiar with a pool, you will learn the location of its *lies*. Lies are positions in the pool where the salmon can rest a day or more while running. A lie must provide the fish with a good flow of well-oxygenated water while requiring minimal energy for the fish to maintain its position. The fish must also have unobstructed access to deep water. Lies may be associated with a gravel bar, a rock or ledge, a sunken log, or some other impediment to the current. However, these features do not necessarily produce lies, because they may not, for one reason or another, fulfill the salmon's subtle requirements. On the other hand, a minor depression in the gravel, such as an eel's nest, may allow the fish to hold there with little effort. Lies may endure for many years, but they can be lost overnight during the spring breakup. Gravel and large rocks may shift, destroying some lies while simultaneously creating others. After a hard winter, a pool may fish quite differently than it did the previous season. In the extreme, a pool may completely fill with gravel.

Lies that hold fish at normal water levels may not do so during higher flows. High water may also produce new holding areas. A slack-water pond in the river, which rarely holds fish at normal water levels, may have a moderate flow while the rest of the river is a torrent, and may be the only place to fish.

Considering the concentration of salmon on them, it might seem sensible to fish *only* the lies. However, there are good reasons to cover the entire pool. As we've said, lies may appear and disappear in a single winter. You can discover such changes only by covering the water thoroughly at the start of each season. Even a small rise in water level may promote a new lie or downgrade one that had been producing a few days before.

Salmon most often take a fly when they are about to run, or just after they have stopped running. Occasionally they will leave their lies to cruise the pool. These forays provide you with opportunity to take them where no lies exist. During overcasts, or at above-average water levels, fish will move upstream almost continuously, with only a few minutes' rest after ascending falls or rapids. You may take them then from areas that are not normally lies. You may also encounter running fish as they move up a pool after having rested in its tail.

STRATEGIES

Typical Pools

Figure 4-5 shows a typical salmon pool and the locations of its lies. Imagine you approach the pool from upstream. Deep water close to the right bank prevents you from wading that side. You must fish from the shingle, or by wading the left-bank shallows. The rock protruding from the deep water near the top, and the ledge below it, look like locations where fish may lie. You are tempted to position yourself at the neck of the pool so that when you cast at a 45-degree angle to the current, your fly will swing just in front, and to the side of the rock. All very well, but if you were to do this, your fly line and its shadow would pass over the top of the bar, which is a less obvious but equally likely position for a lie. This could frighten any fish in the area and put them off taking flies for a considerable time. The proper thing to do is to first move farther back in the neck and cover the water just below the bar by casting at a 10- to 15-degree angle to the current.

Casting to a fish that may be lying by the ledge takes a different strategy. The lie in the tail area that appears as a shallow depression in the river bottom is almost impossible to anticipate unless you have taken a number of fish there previously. If you cast from the edge of the shallows to cover the ledge lie, you will be tempted to do so from a position directly opposite the lie to minimize the length of your casts. But this may bring you so close to the fish in the shallow

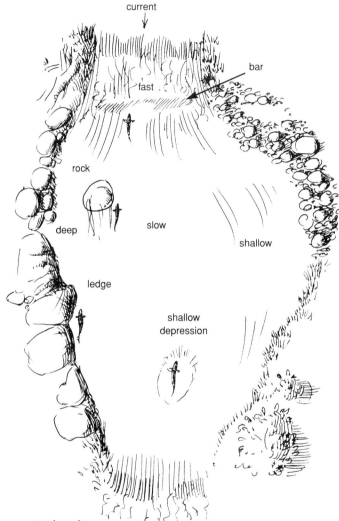

current

bar

fast

rock

deep

slow

shallow

ledge

shallow
depression

FIGURE 4-5. *Salmon lies in a typical pool.*

depression that you spook it. However, if you first explore the entire tail area with a series of short casts from positions close to shore, you will not disturb any fish on the ledge, and you can work the ledge once you've dealt with the tail. By spending a little time thinking about the situation you may have doubled your chance of success.

Intensity of Coverage

How many times should you cover a pool before moving on? Much depends on your temperament, the availability of other pools, and your judgment of their quality. If a pool has produced for you in the past, you will fish it with confidence and close attention.

Without question, your first pass down the pool in the morning holds your greatest chance for success. Each subsequent pass introduces the possibility that the salmon holding in it have been frightened, and thus are less likely to take. However, it is possible to take your first fish on your fourth pass, and perhaps another fish thereafter.

Beginners' Errors

Some beginning salmon anglers concentrate their efforts on the deepest sections of a pool. As they become more familiar with its lies, they will find this is not always a good approach. A pool's depths often flow too slowly to supply salmon with the necessary oxygen. Moreover, it is unlikely a salmon will rise through 9 feet (2.8 meters) or more of water to take a fly. There is a large, deep pool on the Matane where Trout River enters the main stream. You can often find 20 or more salmon resting there. Casting over these fish with any type of fly is almost invariably unproductive. However, if you cast over the relatively shallow water at the pool's two heads and at its tail, you will have better luck, particularly on a cloudy day when some of the fish are running. The same is true for any deep pool. When covering them, focus most of your attention on the head and tail. Such a pool is depicted in Figure 4-9. The water is at least 20 feet (6 meters) deep in the center. The salmon lie in depths of 2 to 4 feet (0.6 to 1.2 meters) at the head and tail.

Some beginners refrain from fishing fast flows. This stems from their ignorance of the great disparity between the surface velocity of a run and the velocity along its bottom. While the surface flow may be much too strong for a fish to hold position there, the velocity near the bottom might be quite reasonable, particularly if it contains depressions or rocks, which allow the salmon to hold its position with minimal effort. A good guide is aware of these areas and will point them out.

Fish the fast flow at the head of a pool carefully. Salmon about to leave the pool will linger there before moving out in the evening. While this may not be the best taking location in the pool, it does offer an opportunity you should not ignore, particularly if fish are scarce.

The Fish in the "Bathtub"

The salmon's preference for lies means that it may be found in any part of the pool that constitutes a lie. Keep this in mind, particularly when fishing unfamiliar pools. One evening I arrived at a favorite pool to find it occupied by three other anglers. There was no time to move to another pool, so I took a position in the shallows below the tail, hoping someone would leave early and I could take his place for a few casts before nightfall. While waiting I practiced casting. To make it more interesting, I tried putting a fly as close as possible to a prominent groove on the surface some 50 feet (15 meters) in front of me. I was more than a little surprised when a fish boiled on my fly. My inclination was to cast again immediately, but considering how few options I had if this failed, I decided to first rest the fish. After five minutes passed, I cast again with the original fly, which the fish took solidly. After releasing the fish, I waded over and found it had been lying in a bathtub-sized hole. I looked for the hole the next year, but it had filled in during the winter.

It is best to start fishing unfamiliar pools from the bank, or at least by wading close to the bank. In a strange pool it is quite possible to wade down through a group of lies, spooking their occupants, while casting to barren water. Suppose you are fishing the bank of a pool whose head is entered by a coldwater brook (Figure 4-7). In a slow current, the cold water will flow downstream along the bank for a good bit before it mixes completely with the main stream. You can demonstrate this by taking the river's temperature as you walk down the edge of the pool. The temperature will gradually rise as you move downstream, but the difference will be appreciable for a surprising distance. Any salmon in the pool will likely be lying in this cooler strip. Only after covering this bank thoroughly should you even consider wading it to fish the rest of the pool.

Pools with Two Currents

The pool in Figure 4-6 presents a different set of problems. This pool is long and deep. A large rock (A) at the head splits the two currents with a stretch of dead water (between the dotted lines). At normal flows, the tops of rocks A, B, and F are well out of the water, while rocks C, D, E, and G are submerged. A fish that has just negotiated a long stretch of rapids and has entered the pool will often take up a lie (or perhaps just a resting spot, where it will remain for only a few minutes) in the tail, and a favorite place to do this is at the river side and to the rear of rock F. However, I advise you to cover the whole tail with care, because fish can be taken almost anywhere. The reason for this, I believe, is

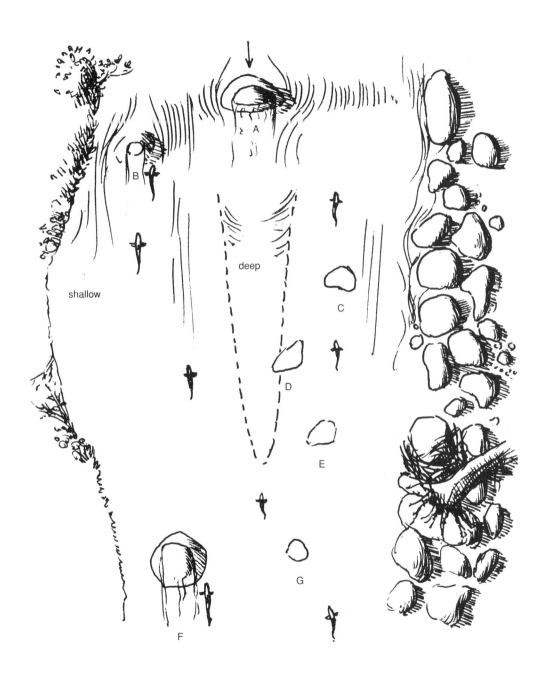

FIGURE 4-6. *Salmon lies in a pool with two currents.*

ROTATION FISHING

Rotation fishing allows a large number of rods to fish a single pool equitably. Rather than forming a stationary line from head to tail, with each rod fishing a little slice of water, everyone moves down one step after each cast. Once an angler reaches the tail, he has the option of taking time out to change his fly or going directly back to the head to start a new circuit. This way an angler fishes the entire pool.

Each location will have specific rules to deal with different events. If you raise a fish, for example, you might be allowed a set number of casts, often five, before you are required to move along. In some lines you are allowed one change of fly. The angler who hooks a fish is usually allowed some latitude in playing time but is encouraged to work the fish hard to minimize it.

On a small pool that can accommodate only one rod at a time, the angler is allowed, say, ten minutes of fishing time, after which he goes to the end of the line.

Rotation fishing doesn't offer the best chances of hooking a fish but the social aspects and good-natured commentary of the group when a fish is being played offer some compensation.

twofold: (1) salmon are stopping to "get their breath" after their ascent of the rapids, and (2) they must decide which of the two currents they will use to move up the pool. In making their decision, they move about a good deal, testing the water. If the fish chooses the right current (facing downstream), it may pause near rock B before leaving the pool. Fish are difficult to reach here because the cast must be at least 70 feet (21 meters) long and must be mended. This is a deep pool, and you can wade only from the left shore, not more than 20 feet (6 meters) from the shingle, and only when the river is well down. At one time there was a very productive lie at rock E, but this was lost to heavy ice a few years back. In the autumn (and rarely in summer), fish will rest along the dotted lines. In the fall the salmon, for some unknown reason, prefer the right-hand current, which is of course the more difficult to fish.

Pools with Tributary Water

Figure 4-7 shows a coldwater brook entering a salmon river whose temperature is in the mid-70s F (low 20s C). Salmon cannot survive for long at this temperature, so they crowd into the tongue of cold water exiting the brook,

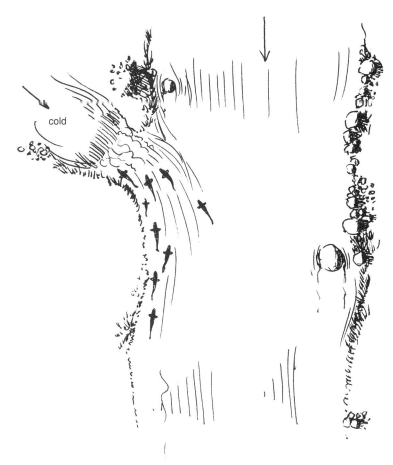

cold

FIGURE 4-7. *Influence of tributary water on salmon locations.*

which may be running at 52 degrees F (11 degrees C). But suppose the main stream is running at 70 degrees F (21 degrees C). Salmon can tolerate this temperature, but they much prefer a cooler location. Under these circumstances they probably will pass up good lies in the main part of the pool to take positions in the coldwater tongue. Salmon will not crowd this area, however, because at this temperature their running will not be completely halted.

If the two streams are of comparable size and temperature, chances are good you'll find fish along the broken line where their waters converge. Some anglers have suggested the salmon pause here to compare the odors of the two branches so they may choose the one leading to their birthplace. This makes sense to me.

MOVING ABOUT THE RIVER

Wading for salmon is no different from wading for trout—except that the rivers are, in general, bigger and more powerful. Consequently, a mistake can get you into more serious trouble. Almost all neophyte salmon anglers have had some trout fishing experience, and the few who have not probably will be starting out with a guide to keep them out of trouble or ferry them around the river in a canoe—the preferred river craft. The superb canoe handling of a Miramichi guide working his way down a rapid with a pole is a skill dying out for lack of recruits among the younger generation.

The Two-Angler Team

In certain circumstances two anglers can work as a team, increasing their chances of success. On a bright, calm day, one angler can take a position above the river and observe the fish's reaction to flies through polarized sunglasses. Over a light-colored bottom, the salmon's dark back makes it highly visible, especially in a slow flow. But they are more difficult to spot over a dark gravel bottom. The trick is to look for the white inside the fish's mouth, which appears and disappears rhythmically as it breathes. Find the flashing white spot and you will then see the fish's outline. You can now instruct your partner how to best present his fly. Frequently the fish will be unmoved. But at some stage it may show interest, however slight. Such insight is unknown to the solitary angler, who may well conclude the lie is unoccupied. Short of hooking the fish, or prompting a rise, the only way for the angler to know there is a fish there at all is to get above the pool and scout it before casting. Two anglers working together increase the chances of each other's success.

Fishing from a Canoe

You can fish large pools most efficiently from a canoe (Figure 4-8). Starting from an anchored position at the head, make a short cast to one side of the canoe. Then, with the same length of line, cast to the other side. Lengthen the line a bit and cast again. Then cast to the other side. Continue to lengthen line after every other cast until you've made the longest cast you are capable of within the pool's limits. Now raise the *killick* (anchor) momentarily, allowing the canoe

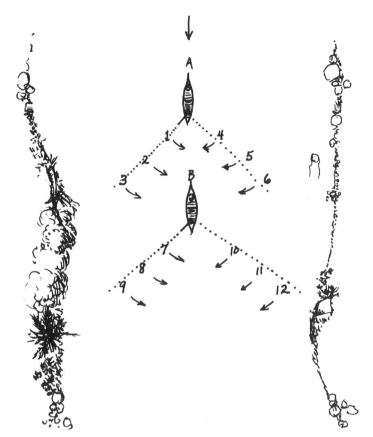

FIGURE 4-8. *Covering a large pool with casts from a canoe.*

to move downstream far enough that you can cover new water the same way. Just as if you were wading, you can vary the intensity of your coverage by changing the distance between casts and the length of the drops. Many large pools can be covered adequately only by canoe. There are drawbacks to boat fishing, however. The steel-shod pike pole used to move the canoe causes a good deal of underwater noise. The killick makes underwater noise as well, especially as it is dislodged from rocks. Most anglers prefer to have their feet on firm ground. Of course, if a large fish gets you deep into your backing, it is easier to handle this from a canoe, as the guide can chase the fish and allow you to recover line. If the salmon hangs up on a rock or submerged log, you have a much better chance of freeing it from a boat than you would while wading. When I am fishing from a canoe I usually prefer the guide to take me ashore once I've hooked a fish.

FIGURE 4-9. *Salmon prefer the head and tail of a deep pool.*

DEALING WITH ABORTED TAKES

Resting Fish and Changing Flies

Sometimes the salmon's move to the fly is tentative. You see no swirl, but only the bright-silver flash as the fish turns on its side. Your reaction should be to cast again—and again—each at the exact same distance and at the same angle to the current. However, repeated casts often fail to elicit a response from a fish that has shown an interest. When this happens, tradition tells us to change to a smaller size of the same fly, or to a different pattern entirely. Quite often this is effective, but only, in my opinion, because changing flies takes time. I believe the time it takes to change flies builds up tension in the fish. If we accept that this delay is at least partially responsible for the fish's increased interest, it hardly seems reasonable to get rid of a fly in which the fish has already shown interest. Only after you have given the original pattern an intensive trial, in various sizes and degrees of dressing (sparseness and fullness) should you consider changing patterns. Even then, the new pattern should differ from the original in only a single feature (see Chapter 7).

Low-Water Patterns

If you tie your own flies, dress them in varying degrees of fullness. It's surprising how much difference this can make, particularly with fish located in slow water. Here I might advise you to show them a *low-water pattern*. Low-water patterns are dressed on fine-wire hooks. The dressing occupies the forward half of the hook, giving you a small fly with the hooking and holding ability of a much larger tie. The dressing is often simplified and reduced. The wing may consist of as few as a dozen hairs, and the hackle may only be two or three wisps at the throat. Since the dressing is well forward of the hook point, the fly is better able to hook fish that nip, as they often do in low water. The pattern doesn't seem to make much difference; the salmon are apparently more attracted by the slight silhouette than by any details of the dressing.

While changing flies, do not be in a hurry to get back to the fish. Unless it is almost dark, it will not leave its lie to move upriver.

full   sparse   low water

FIGURE 4-10. *The same fly dressed full, sparse, and as a low-water pattern.*

The Best Times to Fish

As we've said, salmon are most likely to take a fly just after they have stopped running, or just as they are about to run. This indicates early morning and evening as prime fishing times. Wind, inevitable on salmon rivers, often starts at mid-morning and continues until late afternoon, dying down again toward evening. At each end of the day the fish are in a better taking mood. A good general rule is to start your evening fishing only after the sun is off the water. In the early morning, the fish are settling into the pools and finding their lies; in the evening they are stirring in preparation to run. Don't be in a hurry to leave the water during the evening. Even on a moonless night salmon can see the smallest flies, and the fishing seems to improve as total darkness approaches. However, I always cease fishing before it gets too dark to land and release fish properly—particularly if I am fishing alone.

On comparing notes with other anglers, you may learn they rose fish close to the same time as you did, introducing the possibility there was something favorable about the time of day. One morning I approached Cap Seize, a large, deep pool on the Matane, to find it occupied by a few active anglers, and many more inactive ones on the bank who informed me that the pool had been dead since before sunrise. As we discussed the possible reasons for this, we heard the splash of a hooked fish. Before this salmon could be brought to net, a second was hooked. And in the next half hour, more than a dozen fish were landed by the 20-plus rods in the pool. Then things quieted. These short-lived periods of excellent fishing do not occur often, and I have heard no convincing explanation as to their impetus.

Effects of Light and Weather

On a bright day the quality of the fishing generally falls off the higher the sun gets in the sky. Certainly one reason for this is that on a bright day you have more chance of scaring the fish. The fly line, both during casting and while floating on the water's surface, casts a shadow the salmon associates with danger. Sunny afternoons are better used for activities other than salmon fishing, at least until late afternoon, when the sun's angle to the water decreases.

An overcast day gives the salmon angler two advantages: diminished shadows and, more often than not, calm weather. On overcast days you can usually fish all day long. Of course, it's possible you might be rained on. But a little rain doesn't bother the fish, and if you have a good rain jacket, a summer shower should not deter you. A downpour can complicate things, however, wetting your glasses and causing them to steam. You can prevent your glasses from getting wet by wearing a fishing hat with a long visor.

Overcasts encourage fish to run continuously, particularly if the flow is higher than normal. Overcasts require a change in your strategy because there will be fewer fish on the usual lies. As we've said, your best chance to take them is when they pause to rest after running a difficult section of water.

A thunderstorm is a different matter. Thunder will put the fish down. In addition, graphite conducts electricity, and is an excellent target for lightning. When lightning starts, get out of the water and wait for the storm to pass. As soon as it does, get back on the river—the fish are often active after a thunderstorm.

THINGS TO AVOID

Avoid sloppy casts at all times—they scare fish—particularly when approaching a lie. When the sky is filled with passing clouds, I wait until one of them obscures the sun before casting to a lie (that is, if the wait is not unreasonable).

Move as quietly as possible both in the water and on the banks, particularly over rocks. Sounds travel faster and farther through water than through air, and are believed to disturb salmon and put them off flies.

Having made all these generalizations, I feel it necessary to again point out that the salmon is an unpredictable creature. The only certainty is that it will violate every rule ascribed to it. I have had fish take my fly at high noon on a bright, cloudless day after a blank morning and a fishless evening the night before. Such mysteries keep me going back to the rivers.

CHAPTER 5

Dry Flies

Origins and Development

In contrast to the many hundreds of wet-fly dressings, there are scarcely more than a few dozen commonly used salmon dry flies. This is due in part to the salmon dry fly's relatively recent appearance. Dry-fly fishing for salmon didn't begin until the early twentieth century, whereas the salmon wet fly dates back at least to 1659, as first described in the second edition of Thomas Barker's *The Art of Angling* (Taverner, 1948). Also, the wet fly affords the angler faster, more thorough coverage of a pool than does a dry fly.

There are scattered reports of salmon being caught with dry flies in Great Britain during the nineteenth century, though the method never caught on in Europe. The British salmon season opens as early as February on some rivers, with water temperatures scarcely above freezing. In earlier times, little fishing was done in Britain past May, by which time water temperatures were high enough to make the large wet flies then used fairly ineffective. Later experience in Canada showed that the conditions best suited for use of the dry and the wet fly overlap, but basically the dry fly is best used at normal to high water temperatures. The inactivity of British salmon anglers during summer, when dry flies would have been most productive, is often cited as one reason this approach was neglected in Britain. But there is a body of evidence suggesting British salmon simply will not take a conventional dry fly consistently.

Atlantic salmon fishing in North America could not begin in February, and in the early years fishing ceased here too as the water warmed in early summer. It wasn't until the 1930s, when Ira Gruber showed salmon could be taken in low, warm water using small wet flies (to size 12), that summer fishing was seriously pursued. Earlier, in the years 1914 to 1918, three Americans—Colonel Ambrose Monell, George LaBranche, and Edward R. Hewitt—fishing on New Brunswick's Upsalquitch River had worked out the technique and patterns to take salmon on a dry fly. LaBranche detailed this period in his book *The Salmon and the Dry Fly* (first published in 1924), and Hewitt related it in his 1922 book *Secrets of the Salmon* (which was combined with his 1926 book *Telling on the Trout* and published in 1950 in a revised edition titled *A Trout and Salmon Fisherman for Seventy-Five Years*).

The principal locale of the trio's studies was the Forks Pool, lying at the juncture of the Upsalquitch's northwest and southeast branches. They set aside a small section for dry-fly fishing only. LaBranche described it as "a swift steady current about three feet deep, dropping off into deep water at the edge of the pool." The water's surface ran furrowed, each crease spaced about an inch (2.5

centimeters) apart. Salmon lay beneath; occasionally one would leap, or break the surface with its snout. But there was no way of knowing under which furrow a fish might be. One angler at a time cast while the others offered "gratuitous advice." Eventually it became clear that only one of these furrows produced fish. The reason, they finally learned, was because the fish were lined up next to submerged ledge, and the productive strip of water was 4 to 5 inches (10 to 12.7 centimeters) from its edge. If the fly were cast any closer to the ledge, the fish could not see it, and apparently they would not rise to a fly outside the strip. From these observations the three anglers concluded that the fly had to pass within an inch (2.5 centimeters) of the salmon's position. We now know their conclusion is not all-encompassing, since salmon often move considerable distances from their lies to take dry flies. The three were misled by the peculiarities of that particular piece of water.

Their second decree was that the fly should never drag. To accomplish this they fished downriver, pulling back on the rod after the cast had unrolled to drop a length of loose line in front of them as is done in trout fishing. This idea too has subsequently been refuted, for as we shall see in Chapter 6, dragging a commotion-type fly on the surface over a salmon can sometimes be very effective.

The anglers' third belief was that the fly must ride well up on its hackle points—no mean feat without modern flotants—for they observed that fish would rarely take a partially submerged fly. Again their conclusion has since been amended: We now have a number of effective salmon dry flies, notably the Bomber and Lee Wulff's Surface Stonefly, designed to be fished partially submerged.

When the anglers first began their studies, only trout dry flies were available. But during that first winter, LaBranche began developing a number of dry flies specifically for salmon. Believing the fly must float high, he hackled them heavily. LaBranche had no access to selectively bred hackle, so he made do with what he could get from a local chicken farmer. He knew dyeing the hackle caused it to absorb water more readily, so he restricted himself to natural browns and grays. Wings were omitted because they absorbed too much water. The resulting flies were quite similar to the Bivisible trout fly (which was invented by Hewitt, and which attained considerable popularity as a salmon fly). By the start of the second season LaBranche had devised 10 patterns, all of whose hackles were palmered to provide maximum flotation. The Colonel Monell (Figure 5-1) is characteristic of the series, in which the salmon angler's interest is now purely historical.

FIGURE 5-1. *The Colonel Monell; see Plate 1 for dressing instructions.*

Flies were not the only equipment the anglers revised. Monell designed a new rod to present dry flies more delicately. Although it was a 14-foot (4.2 meters) two-handed rod, it was a great improvement over the larger sticks then used.

The gut leaders of the time were woefully weak compared with today's nylon monofilament (Table 5-1), and had to be fairly large in diameter to hold a salmon—which did nothing to effect a delicate presentation. The only advantages these anglers had over us were the large numbers of salmon with little sport-fishing pressure.

TABLE 5-1

Relative Strength of Nylon Monofilament and Silkworm Gut

Diameter (inches)	Pound Test	
	Gut	Nylon*
0.012	4–4.5	10
0.010	3–3.5	8
0.008	2–2.5	5

*A standard tippet material widely used in salmon fishing.

Despite the writings of Hewitt and LaBranche, the salmon-angling community was slow to use dry flies. In 1929 Lee Wulff began tying his namesake series of dry flies, which were attractive to salmon and less water-absorbent than the LaBranche flies. The Wulff dry flies and their progeny (including Dan Bailey's variations of the original series and Ken Lockwood's Salmon Irresistible; see the Royal Wulff in Plate 4), together with advances in bamboo rod design and the post-war availability of nylon monofilament, made dry-fly fishing for salmon increasingly feasible.

On my first salmon fishing trip, in 1958, I was hard put to learn the wet-fly approach, let alone to learn how to fish dry flies. My instructor and guide, Sharp Pond, was close to retirement then, and was not of a mind to concern himself with floaters, which he and many other guides still regarded with suspicion. One day as we were coming in from the home pool for lunch, I noticed the angler in the canoe in front of ours had left a dry fly dangling over the side of his vessel. The Royal Wulff was bouncing along the surface, hardly more than a leader's length from the rod tip, when suddenly a salmon took the fly with a loud splash. The guide grabbed the rod lest it be pulled overboard, and handed it to his client, who succeeded in landing the fish. The incident left me with an abiding confidence in dry flies. Sharp Pond was unmoved, however, dismissing the incident by saying there was always a crazy fish that would take any fly you put on the water. Many times since I have longed for such a fish.

MODERN DRY FLIES AND TACTICS

Whether or not you fish with dry flies depends much on the water temperature, since dry-fly fishing for salmon is generally better when the water is above 65 degrees F (18 degrees C) and success with wet flies diminishes as the temperature approaches 70 degrees F (21 degrees C). (High temperatures often coincide with low water, but not always.) Thus, for morning fishing you might use wet flies until the water temperature reaches the mid-60s F (around 18 degrees C), after which you might switch to dry flies. You might also take the fish's behavior into consideration in choosing which type of fly to fish. Very often, porpoising fish will prefer dry flies; jumping fish, on the other hand, show no such preference. There are no hard-set rules, however; you can catch salmon in 50-degree F (10-degree C) water with a dry fly and in 70-degree F (21-degree C) water with a small wet fly. Your options to fishing either straight wet flies or dry flies are to fish wet flies with a Portland hitch (Figure 6-1) or to use a commotion fly (Chapter 6). When one method is not working, perhaps a different approach will better suit the fish's mood.

Occasionally salmon will show a preference for a very small dry fly. At these times a few trout patterns, such as Spiders and Variants in sizes 10 or 12, will do the job provided they are dressed on wire heavy enough to deal with salmon.

You can fish conventional dry flies such as the Wulffs much the same way for salmon as you would for trout, simply allowing them to dead-drift over the fish. One of the simplest and most effective dry flies is the MacIntosh. It consists of a sparse floss body, a long, thick wing of fox-squirrel tail fastened at the middle of the hook shank and extending well beyond the bend, and two brown saddle hackles wound forward to the eye. It floats well, due as much to the wing as to the hackles. It lies low in the water, both the hackle and wing fibers penetrating the surface film. One day, while casting repeatedly over a fish that had boiled on my MacIntosh without taking, I was surprised to see the dorsal fin of another salmon cutting rapidly across the pool toward my fly. The fish hit the fly at full speed. Perhaps it reacted to the sound of the fly landing on the water, since it had to be well out of the fish's sight at the time.

Two of the standard salmon dry flies have spun-deer-hair bodies: the Salmon Irresistible (adapted from the trout fly) and the Rat-Faced MacDougall. The latter was a great favorite of Fred Clowater, who guided at Jack Russell's Camp when I was learning to fish for salmon. Since my own guide, Sharp Pond, was disdainful of dry flies, I approached Fred for his advice on a dry pattern I could use when I fished the home pool alone after supper. He strongly recommended a Rat-Faced MacDougall, and after several evenings I took my first dry-fly-caught salmon, a grilse, with it. I'm sure word got back to Sharp, but neither he nor I ever mentioned it.

Herb McKay, my longtime guide on the Miramichi, had a great collection of stories, one of which involves the Rat-Faced MacDougall. Herb was guiding an older woman on her first salmon-fishing trip. Her limited casting skills prevented her from having any success at all. One day Herb noticed a fish porpoising quite close to the canoe. He tied a Rat-Faced MacDougall to the woman's tippet and instructed her to wave a yard or two of line over where he had seen the breaking fish. At his command, she let the fly settle on the surface. The salmon promptly came on with a rush and made off with the fly in the corner of its mouth. After a long battle, the woman finally brought the fish to net. She was ecstatic, and wanted to head back to camp immediately to proclaim her victory. On the way back she asked Herb the name of the fly, and where she could buy one. Herb sent her to MacCluskey's, the general store in Boisetown. When the young clerk behind the counter, one of the MacCluskey boys, asked how he could help her, the woman stammered, "Oh dear. I want a Rat-Faced . . . a Rat-Faced . . . " and then smiling triumphantly, "I want a Rat-Faced MacCluskey." To which the boy replied without pause: "Well ma'am, I'm available, but maybe you'd be more comfortable with the old man."

You can fish such flies as Whiskers, Bombers, and Buck Bugs either as conventional dry flies or as commotion flies—that is, skittered across the surface to produce a wake. Commotion flies are discussed in Chapter 6.

Fly Placement

The important question in fishing dry flies is, "Where should I place the fly?" Fishing a large pool with a dry fly takes more time than it does with a wet fly simply because each dry-fly float covers less water. On a small pool the difference is trivial, but on a large pool it can be important. On the other hand, if you are familiar with a large pool and its lies, you can concentrate on known hot spots with a dry fly. You might fish up the pool with a dry fly—this method disturbs fish the least—and then downstream with a wet fly.

Downstream Casting

A variation on traditional dry-fly presentation was developed by Jack Russell (1951), a method he called *downstream casting*. While standing in an anchored canoe, strip line off your reel, coil it at your feet, and make a long cast downstream without shooting the line. When the current removes the slack from your cast, feed additional line through the guides fast enough to prevent drag. When you get to the end of your fly line, retrieve it in foot-long pulls. Modern flotants will allow you to do this without drowning your fly. This method keeps your fly on the water much longer than do any of the conventional casts. I have seen it used successfully at the Russell camp, but seldom use it myself as I don't enjoy fishing from a canoe, though I suppose you could use it for some wading situations as well.

Teasing Fish

Teasing a salmon with a dry fly will sometimes evoke a strike. This method, which I believe originated on Quebec's Matane River, is sometimes useful when casting to playful fish, or to fish that can be seen on their lie but refuse to rise (Figure 5-2). The object is to give the fish a glimpse of the fly in various parts of its window[1], but not allow it enough time to respond before you pick the fly up and deliver it to another location. You can place the fly to either side of the fish (the crosses in Figure 5-2; their distance from the fish depends on the fish's depth, i.e., the size of its window). You can include a teasing float from directly above the fish, taking the fly away when it reaches point A. All this activity presumably builds tension in the fish, so that when the fly is finally allowed to float over the fish's lie, the fish will react violently and without caution. The method sometimes works, but, as with all other approaches in salmon fishing, sometimes it doesn't. If you are faced with a difficult fish, teasing it is certainly worth trying. I once watched an angler on the Matane take about 20 minutes to tease a fish lying over a ledge. When he finally presented the fly over the ledge,

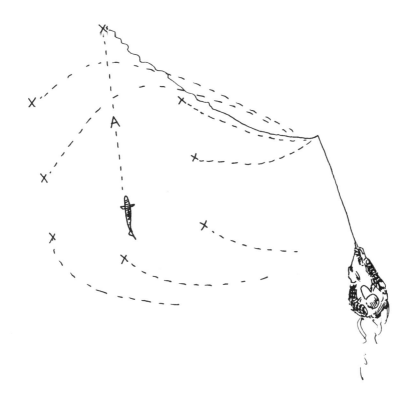

FIGURE 5-2. *Casting pattern of a dry fly used to build tension in a salmon.*

the fish started to move to the fly, but then thought better of it and returned to its lie. I moved on to another pool. When I returned, the angler said he had caught the fish after another episode of teasing.

The Dry Fly as a Locator

For locating fish with a dry fly, Lee Wulff recommended a size-1 White Wulff, aptly called the Seagull. He wrote that fish will often rise to such a fly without taking it. He then used a smaller dry fly to elicit a strike. The Seagull (about as large as a hummingbird, according to Wulff) is somewhat difficult to cast. A large White Bomber is much easier to present and serves the same purpose.

Sometimes a fish will swirl at your wet fly, but then refuse subsequent wet flies. After you've shown the fish a number of wet flies in various sizes, offer it a dry fly or a commotion fly before giving up.

The Salmon's Rise to a Dry Fly

The great attraction of dry-fly fishing for salmon is the thrill of the surface take. At times salmon will come clear out of the water with the fly in their mouth. This great rush is deceptive, however, and may be your undoing if you react to it as you would to a trout's rise. For all its commotion, the salmon's rise to a dry fly is still more leisurely than the deft slurp of a hungry brown trout. The sight of a salmon coming mouth-open at a floating fly can make you anxious, resulting in your pulling the fly cleanly from the fish's mouth. Don't give the fish too much time to reject the fly, however. Usually, setting the hook just as the fish starts to descend with the fly in its mouth will do the job—but not even experienced salmon anglers get it right every time.

Salmon do not always take a dry fly with a rush. At times they rise with their mouth closed and bump it with their head or miss it entirely. Other times they hit it with their tail as if to sink it. This most often happens while fishing with a Bomber, but it may occur with any dry fly. When this happens with a Bomber, changing to a different body or hackle color sometimes produces a take. Twitching the fly an inch or two as it enters the fish's window can also be helpful. A smaller fly, or one with a radically different silhouette, such as a Spider or Skater, may also work. As a last resort, rest the fish for 10 to 15 minutes before casting again. Nobody knows why salmon act so exasperatingly. Perhaps they are not completely fooled by the fly, but cannot entirely suppress their reflexive urges.

Note

1. As light waves pass through the air and hit water, they bend. Thus, fish have a restricted view of objects outside the water and on its surface. The fish's limited view of the surface and beyond is termed its *window*. Outside the perimeter of this circular window the fish sees only a reflection of the river bottom. The diameter of the window depends on the depth of the fish. At a depth of 6 feet (1.8 meters), the fish's window measures 66 inches (1.7 meters) in diameter; at a depth of a foot (30.5 centimeters), the window is a mere 10 inches (25.4 centimeters).

CHAPTER 6

Commotion Flies

A S DEFINED BY FATHER ELMER J. SMITH, A COMMOTION FLY IS one that attracts salmon by commotion as it moves across the water's surface. As we shall see, this concept is not new, but it has received much attention since the 1960s with the appearance of Father Smith's Bombers and the similar Buck Bugs. The impact of these flies on salmon fishing has been so substantial we may consider them a separate class of flies lying somewhere between wet and dry flies. Since commotion flies are defined by function, we may include any fly presented to disturb the surface during at least some part of its ride.

THE RIFFLING HITCH

The Portland Creek riffling hitch has a long history in salmon fishing, and survives to this day on most salmon rivers as an effective alternative to traditional wet-fly presentation. In his classic book *The Atlantic Salmon*, Lee Wulff described the origin of the riffling hitch on Newfoundland's Portland Creek, where he once owned salmon-fishing camps. Many years ago, Wulff wrote, officers of British warships anchored off the coast would often come ashore to fish the Creek. The salmon flies of the day were dressed on eyeless hooks with a loop of gut whipped to the front of the shank by which it could be fastened to the leader. With use, this gut loop eventually would deteriorate. Rather than lose a fish to a bad loop, officers gave their well-used flies to the local anglers. The guides soon discovered the pitfall of these gifts, but learned to avoid losing fish by throwing a couple of half hitches around the shank behind the head of the fly after tying the fly to the leader. This not only strengthened the fly's attachment to the leader, but it also caused the fly to skitter across the water's surface on its side. A hitched fly produced well—so well, in fact, there was a time when guides at Wulff's Portland Creek Camp hitched all their wet flies, convinced they caught more fish than unhitched flies.

To riffle hitch a fly, tie it on as you would any other fly, and then take two half hitches behind the fly's head so that the second hitch leaves the monofilament pointing down for double-hooked flies, or at 45 degrees to one side for single-hooked flies (Figure 6-1). For single-hooked flies the hitch should come off the same side of the fly as the direction in which the water is flowing. That is, if the water is flowing to your right, the hitch should come off the fly's right side so that the hook point is downstream.[1]

The speed at which a hitched fly moves relative to the water's surface is crit-

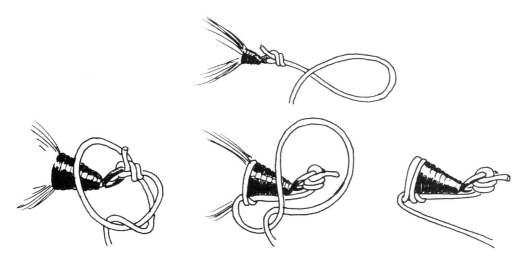

FIGURE 6-1. *Tying a Portland hitch on a wet fly. From* Atlantic Salmon Fishing *by L. James Bashline.*

ical. If it moves too fast it throws water; if it moves too slowly it sinks. Properly fished, the fly produces a wake across the surface that is most attractive to salmon. This necessitates adjusting the fly's speed by taking in or releasing line during the swim. A salmon often moves to a riffled fly with its dorsal fin cutting the surface. Don't try to make things easier for the fish by slowing the fly—the fish more often than not will lose interest when a riffling fly decelerates.

The riffled-hitch presentation is physically demanding. Constantly having to adjust the fly's speed can be tiring. I recommend using a riffling hitch after you have had a salmon come to your fly but then refuse all subsequent offerings. The hitched fly's wake often provokes a response. It is also a good tactic when fishing heavy currents. Let's say you suspect a fish is lying near a rock situated in a flow so heavy that mending to prevent drag would be fruitless. A conventional wet-fly cast would be futile as well, as the current will belly your line and whip the fly away from the fish before it has a chance to respond. If you can get well above the rock and bring the fly in at a small angle to the current, you might have a chance. A hitched fly moving rapidly on the surface will often cause such an aggressive response that a brief glimpse by the fish is sufficient. At times, a dry fly will also elicit such a take.

You can riffle any wet fly, but those dressed on light-wire hooks work best because they are easier to keep on the surface. I feel the dressing is unimpor-

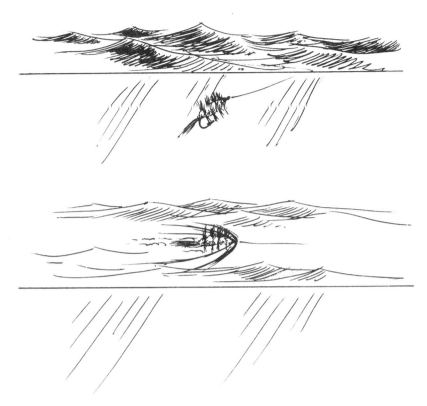

FIGURE 6-2. *A hitched fly produces a noticeable V-wake.*

tant, as the salmon sees little more than the fly's rapidly moving silhouette. The fly's wake, suggestive of an insect or small fish, is likely the impetus for the strike.

Salmon will sometimes move to a riffling fly from quite some distance. Presumably they are reacting more to the wake than to the fly itself: The disruption, it seems, prompts the fish to investigate. Lee Wulff wrote of a salmon that rose to the wake of a leader knot in lieu of his wet fly. When he then rifflehitched the same fly, the fish took it on the second cast. I once had a problem with two salmon lying in the rapid flow of a pool's tail. The fish ignored a variety of wet flies swung a yard or more into the tail. Recalling Wulff's experience, I hitched a fly and presented it in the last bit of smooth water at the tail. The first cast stirred one of the fish, and a repeat cast brought it rushing into the tail to take the fly. The salmon's taking of a hitched fly often rivals its acrobatic rise to a dry fly. As with dry flies, however, there are also occasions when the fish veers off the riffling fly at the last moment.

EARLY COMMOTION FLIES

In the 1930s Edward R. Hewitt invented a commotion fly for trout he called the Neversink Skater, named for the Neversink River in the Catskills, where he had a fishing camp before the city of New York drowned it with a reservoir. The Neversink Skater was tied on a short-shanked hook with large hackle and no tail. The salmon version of the Neversink Skater was tied on larger hooks, and with the largest, stiffest hackle available.

The Skitter Fly, a Miramichi pattern, is also fished in the surface film—either drifted, dragged, or skated. Its brown bucktail wing is tied spinner fashion—slightly tilted back and divided to splay nearly flat. Another Miramichi pattern known as Whiskers was also designed for surface fishing, and has a long history of productivity in many North American rivers. Its fan-shaped wing of deer body hair is fastened on top of the hook shank and faces slightly forward. Essentially, any fly skittered across the surface falls into the category of commotion flies.

THE BOMBER AND THE BUCK BUG

Although the Skitter Fly and Whiskers were worthy forerunners, it wasn't until Father Elmer Smith developed the Bomber that commotion flies gained wide popularity.

One evening in the early 1960s Father Smith joined a group of anglers on the Royal River at Yarmouth, near Portland, Maine, to fish for large sea-run brown trout. These trout were known to be difficult, and the anglers were armed with all the latest equipment and ideas. Nevertheless, they were having no success—and neither was Father Smith. As Father Smith described it, a kid came along with an old beat-up rod bearing a spun-hair mouse fly as a lure. He chucked that hair-mouse out into the river with those high-grade anglers all about him and *crash*—he had on a 10-pound brown trout. Why, Father Smith asked himself, was this hair-mouse attractive to these trout when they had ignored all other offerings? He decided the most obvious difference between the mouse and the other flies was the disturbance it made as it moved. The similarity between sea-run brown trout and Atlantic salmon suggested to Father Smith that such a fly might also work on *Salmo salar*. When he got home, he went straight to his tying vise. He first tied a clump of natural deer body hair at the bend of the hook for a tail, then spun a body. Father Smith knew a full-sized mouse would be too bulky to cast on windy salmon rivers, so he trimmed

FIGURE 6-3. *A Bomber tied by its inventor, Father Elmer J. Smith (see Plate 1).*

the body to a roughly cylindrical shape. Father Smith originally conceived the Bomber as a wet fly, so when he added a hackle, he used a single grizzly hen hackle dyed red, which he tied in by its tip at the bend and palmered forward over the body.

Father Smith first tried the new fly on the Miramichi at Russell Rapids, near Doaktown, New Brunswick. Fishing alone, he cast straight across the fast current, allowing a belly to form in his line. When the line tightened, the fly cut across the flow, moving just beneath the surface. After several such casts, a salmon took the fly with a tremendous boil. The promise offered by the little boy's deer-hair mouse on the Royal River was confirmed. Fly-fishing for salmon would now take a new and fascinating direction.

For a long time Father Smith continued to fish the Bomber subsurface—and with great success. He noticed, however, that fish often struck when the fly was high in the surface film, leaving a wake as it swung through the current. This suggested to him it might be an effective dry fly. He dressed a Dry Version with two stiff saddle hackles tied in by their butts at the hook bend and palmered forward to the eye. You might assume this was done for flotation. Not so. Father Smith asserts that a Bomber doesn't float on its hackle. Instead, he used the hackles to introduce color and to break the surface film. Father Smith found that the Dry Version sometimes requires induced motion during the float to elicit a strike. The amount of motion for a particular lie must be determined by trial. It may vary from one or more twitches to a full strip. As we can see, the distinction between a dry fly and a commotion fly is not always clear.

As with many popular flies, numerous versions of the Bomber have been tied in a variety of color combinations (see Plate 1 for Bomber tied by Father Smith) and styles. Bodies may be white, brown, green, red, yellow, black, or pink; hackles may be brown, orange, grizzly, red, or green. (Use a white body with orange hackle if you have trouble seeing the fly in poor light.) Some Bombers have a deer-hair wing projecting forward from the head. When I interviewed Father Smith for an article on the Bomber (*Atlantic Salmon Journal*, Winter 1990), he did not believe his dressing was sacred. Nevertheless, his 30 years' experience with the fly—he had tied many hundreds for himself and his friends—convinced him that the Dry Version was as productive as any he had fished. The fly in Figure 6-3 he gave me to use as a model. Note the relatively short, bushy tail, the body taper, the hackle spacing, and the absence of a wing.

The Bomber's body is widest over the hook point, so you need a wide gape to ensure solid hookups. Father Smith found his answer in Herter's 3XL Gaelic Supreme, which he considered the finest Bomber hook ever made. Fortunately he acquired a good supply before Herter's went out of business. According to Dick Stewart's *The Hook Book*, the widest-gape 3XL streamer hook presently available is Mustad's 38941. Unfortunately, it is also one of the heaviest. Partridge's D 4A is 10.5 percent lighter than the Mustad with only a small (6 percent) sacrifice in gape.[2]

The only real difference between Bombers and Buck Bugs is that the latter are usually smaller. They are meant to be fished as commotion flies rather than wet (as is usually stated). Buck Bugs have attained great popularity on the Miramichi and other rivers, particularly the version known as the Green Machine (Figure 6-4). As with Bombers, many variations of Buck Bugs exist, including those with fluorescent butts and flash materials.

Buck Bugs can be fished both wet and dry, but they really prove their worth when skittered across the surface to produce a wake. If fished long enough without flotant they will sink, and can then be truly fished as wet flies. This is the choice of some anglers, and there is no question sunken Buck Bugs take fish wet as well. Buck Bugs can also be effective on fish that have refused a series of conventional wet flies.

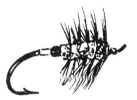

FIGURE 6-4. *The Green Machine.*

BRITISH SALMON AND DRY FLIES

Shortly after George LaBranche published his book *The Salmon and the Dry Fly* in 1924, Arthur H.E. Wood (the originator of greased-line fishing) invited him to demonstrate his methods on the Aberdeenshire Dee, one of Scotland's great salmon rivers. As a crowd of curious anglers gathered, Wood showed LaBranche all the pools and lies. The river ran clear, and everything seemed favorable for his demonstration. But true to form, the salmon were uncooperative. LaBranche rose many fish with his dry flies but hooked none. Wood jested that the fish had lockjaw. In a more serious vein, he later blamed the flies' heavy hackling, which he felt prevented proper hooking. In four seasons spent in Scotland, LaBranche hooked only one salmon on a dry fly. Some years later, Lee Wulff was only a bit more successful (though he was faced with high winds and rain). Thus it was accepted as gospel that Scottish salmon would take a dry fly only on very rare occasions—too rare to make it a sensible approach. Or so it was explained to me when I proposed to try one on Scotland's South Esk in 1962. The British anglers there politely suggested I could not afford to waste precious time. I did spend a few hours at it, though, using Wulff flies and a Rat-Faced MacDougall, but didn't manage to raise a fish, although they were showing in the pool.

Tube Flies

Considering my own angling experiences in Scotland, and those of Americans who had preceded me, I was greatly surprised to discover a book written in 1987 by a Scot, Derek Knowles, titled *Salmon on a Dry Fly.* I found this book a fascinating read. In essence, Knowles says Scottish salmon will take a dry fly as readily as their North American brethren, provided the fly is skittered on the surface (in my terms, this would be a commotion fly). His book tells how he came to tie a *tube fly* he calls the Yellow Dolly. As their name implies, tube flies are dressed on metal or plastic tubes rather than hooks. The inside diameter of the tube is sufficient to allow a tippet to pass through. The hook is then tied on and the tube is slid down the leader until restrained by the hook eye. In Great Britain, small treble hooks are standard. Trebles are illegal in Maine and Canada, where singles, or more frequently doubles are used instead. If the tube is metal, the whole assembly is the equivalent of a weighted fly. Tube flies are used in Britain in the early season (as early as February on some rivers), when the water is barely above freezing and the fly must be fished close to the bottom. Metal tube flies are illegal in North America, where any weight added to the fly is prohibited. A plastic tube fitted with a small light-wire hook is considerably lighter than a conventional wet fly and tends to stay on the surface, especially in faster water.

For his Yellow Dolly, Knowles uses the red insulation from a piece of copper wire as the tube (outside diameter $\frac{1}{16}$ to $\frac{3}{32}$ of an inch [1.6 to 2.4 millimeters]). He ties on two skirts of deer hair (he prefers the tail of a fallow deer, but cites bucktail as the best alternative), one yellow and one black, about $\frac{1}{4}$ inch (6.4 millimeters) apart, flaring them at a 30- to 45-degree angle to the insulation. After trimming, lacquering, overwrapping, and tying off the butts, Knowles extracts the wire core. He then fits the tube with a size-16 treble hook and treats the wings with flotant. Knowles fishes the Yellow Dolly right on the surface, casting it directly across the current and keeping it moving by lifting the rod tip and stripping line as needed. Small tube flies fish much like riffle-hitched flies, but it requires much less effort to keep tubes on the surface. Scottish salmon, which show little interest in conventional dry flies, will take surface-fished tube flies readily. As such, tube flies apparently constitute an important subclass of commotion flies.

After proving the Yellow Dolly in Scotland, Knowles took it to New Brunswick's Miramichi, where he spent a week in the summer of 1985 at Wilson's Camps at McNamee. He fished his Yellow Dolly with little success, raising five fish but landing none. In all fairness to Knowles we should point out he was fishing a river whose water level was descending after a good rise from upstream rains. This means the fish were running rather than resting on their lies. He would locate them with conventional flies, then switch to the Yellow Dolly. In hindsight he realized the running fish likely moved on while he was making the switch. Also, he suspects the Dolly works better with a treble hook than it does with the small singles and doubles he used in Canada.[3]

While in Canada Knowles was introduced to the Bombers and Buck Bugs.

His initial reaction was skeptical. His Canadian guides told him the Bomber was especially valuable when the water is low and warm. This seemed to Knowles to violate the widely held notion that fly size should decrease as water temperature rises. But as the guides explained to him, this applies only to wet flies. Knowles took some Bombers home with him and found Scottish salmon would take them readily—but only when he imparted motion. He had no success at all when he dead-drifted them. As you'll recall, Father Smith found he often had to move the Bomber to make the salmon take. So perhaps the difference between North American and British salmon is not so great after all.

At this writing, the Bomber and the Buck Bug are over 30 years old. Their having survived that long as widely used patterns is testament to the commotion fly's importance to salmon fishing. Perhaps in the future we will see the number of proven commotion patterns grow.

Notes

1. This is discussed in some detail by Art Lee in the *Atlantic Salmon Journal* (Spring 1995).

2 Partridge has announced a hook specifically designed for Bombers, but at this writing it is as yet unavailable.

3. I have fished tube flies in Scotland fitted with a size-14 treble hook. Although it was quite effective, I would not use a treble hook if I planned to release the fish.

CHAPTER 7

Which Fly?

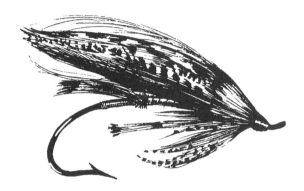

*HAL.—Now I will tell you of another
principle which it is necessary to know, as for
the change of flies for change of weather; I
allude to the different kinds of fly to be used in
particular pools, and even for particular parts
of pools.*

*HAL.—Salmon in this season haunt the
streams in pairs; but so far as rising again after
being pricked, they appear to me to learn when
they have been some time in the river, that the
artificial fly is not food, even without having
been touched by the hook.*

—Sir Humphrey Davy, *Salmonia*

THE TROUT ANGLER CAN MAKE AN INTELLIGENT CHOICE OF FLY pattern by observing the water's prevalent nymphs or terrestrial insects. Since salmon do not feed during their spawning run, we salmon anglers have no such helpful hints to guide us. We are in the position of a trout angler who carries only attractor flies. In the preceding chapters I've made passing reference to the matter of fly selection. I've said that river conditions, such as water height and temperature, are considerations in choosing between a wet or dry fly, and are also considerations in choosing the size of a wet fly. I've also suggested that selecting a fly in which we have confidence will lead to a more successful outcome. We will fish such flies with greater attention to the salmon's tentative responses; and a concentrated effort on a fish that has shown will generally be much more productive than covering new, unknown water.

Why Salmon Take a Fly

Hugh Falkus is a British salmon angler with wide experience on his native rivers. His book *Salmon Fishing: A Practical Guide* is thoughtful, sometimes heretical, but always stimulating. Based on his observations, Falkus has determined six possible motives for salmon to take flies, with which Gary Anderson, a Canadian physician who has written two books on salmon angling, agrees.

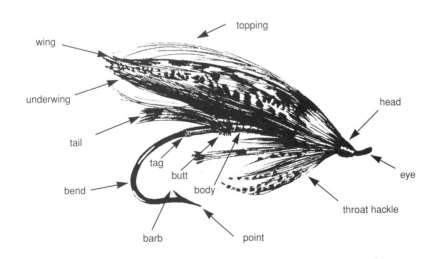

FIGURE 7-1. *The parts of a salmon fly (complex hairwing).*

Feeding Habit

The salmon comes to the fly directly and without hesitation, seizes it, and returns immediately to its lie. Although the fish has no need for food at this stage, or even the means to metabolize it, its feeding instinct is not entirely turned off. This is believed to be the most common motive for the salmon to strike a fly, and the one that gives the angler the best chance of hooking up. Presumably the salmon, finding itself back in the river environment, recalls its parr days, when it fed freely on stream insects. If this is true, a hatchery-raised parr—fed a diet of pellets and stocked in the river as a smolt—would have no recollection of river feeding, and therefore would not take artificial flies as freely when it returned on its spawning run. This may in part explain the unusual reluctance of salmon to take artificial flies in rivers where substantial proportions of the stock are hatchery raised—though this assessment is as yet unproved.

Imagine you are fishing a pool under low-water conditions. You notice that natural insects, too small to be seen easily in the surface film, are being sucked in by fish that you might first mistake for parr. It soon becomes apparent, however, that the rises are quite different from the feeding of those exuberant little fellows, which often jump clear of the water. The insects are being taken with a leisurely subsurface approach and a quiet ingestion. You then wonder if salmon are responsible, even though they are not supposed to feed during their spawning run. A large dorsal fin cuts the surface and your suspicions are strengthened. You will often find these insects to be darkly colored and nymph-like, about size 14. These insects present a rare opportunity to cast to salmon as you would to feeding trout. If you are carrying any dark-colored, size-14 wet flies (any of the Black Bear variations would be suitable) and are willing to play your catch on a light tippet, you are to be commended; for the salmon has a good chance of escaping, and your enjoyment may be limited to seeing the take and briefly feeling the fish's power.[1] A low-water fly will allow you an equally good chance of hooking a fish (salmon do not seem to be hook-shy), and a considerably better chance of landing it. These hatches are brief, and you will be lucky to take more than one salmon, even though a number are rising. The hatch may continue until the group of fish involved (possibly a half-dozen or more) lose interest or pass on upriver.

But what about our dictum that mature salmon do not feed in the river? These fish were certainly taking small flies into their mouth. Professional guides, who have cleaned countless salmon, confirm that almost invariably their stomachs are empty. A few are said to contain a pinkish fluid, and even fewer, some solid material that some guides claim is insect remains. There are a few reports, however, of salmon having been found with their throats crammed with natural insects, often similar to the small dark ones referred to above. When salmon are running, you will occasionally notice a sucking rise undoubtedly due to a salmon; but the fish will have continued upstream before you can even cast. Salmon will take twigs, pieces of bark, and even cigarette butts into their mouth and promptly expel them. I believe they also take natural flies, but we have to presume these are ultimately rejected, since the fish have no use for them: Their digestive system is shut down, and the space is used for storing eggs or milt.

This behavior seems consistent with the proposal that one reason salmon take artificial flies is, being back in the river, they recall their parr days, when they did little else but rise to naturals. It can be seen as an acquired reflex, just as an automobile driver will, without thinking, depress the clutch when he shifts. Grilse generally will take an artificial fly more readily than a two-sea-year fish. The explanation, based on this proposal, is that they have been away from the river one less year and have a more vivid remembrance of parr life.

There is no reason to exclude memories of ocean feeding as a possible motive for salmon to take an artificial fly (Taverner, 1948). Certainly a number of salmon flies are suggestive of small fish. The eminent British salmon angler, Colonel Esmond Drury, developed a fly to simulate a prawn in certain rivers where the use of the natural as bait was forbidden. This rather complex pattern, the General Practitioner, certainly bears more than passing resemblance to a prawn, and is said to be quite effective.

Aggression

Some anglers contend that salmon strike artificial flies out of aggression. Although we noted in Chapter 1 that both male and female salmon exhibit aggressive behavior toward parr on the redds, the adults do not actually harm the parr. So to cite aggression as the motive for salmon seizing artificial flies in the river must be regarded as at least somewhat specious.

A fly that appears suddenly in the fish's window often evokes what seems to be an aggressive take. If we know the fish's position, we can test for alleged aggressive tendencies by placing a fly directly in front of it and then moving the fly rapidly or with commotion. Sometimes a dry fly driven into the water right at a fish's head will provoke a rise. Such a tactic requires either a large bright fly or a commotion fly.

One late-September evening I began fishing by casting a size-4 Orange

Colburn to a likely spot. Just as the fly was about to land, a salmon intercepted it, coming clean out of the water with the fly in its mouth. It was a dark-colored male with a well-developed kype; he was nearly ready to spawn. This certainly seemed to be aggressive behavior.

Inducement

A salmon that follows a wet fly and then takes it after the swing is said to have been *induced.* It is difficult to see how a take at any other point in the fly's swim can be positively identified as inducement, although it may occur without our recognizing it. As often as not, the fish's response is triggered by a slight movement of the fly as the angler prepares for another cast. Perhaps the fish is apprehensive about being lured into shallow water, while at the same time it interprets the fly's movement as an attempt to escape—both incentives for immediate action.

Curiosity

There are exasperating times when salmon will merely nip at a fly rather than take it with more characteristic gusto. I see no reason to believe this behavior is motivated by curiosity. The explanation seems anthropomorphic. Sometimes you can find a fly that will make these nipping salmon take with their usual enthusiasm.

In the fall, after the water temperature has fallen into the 50s (10 to 15 degrees C), the tendency to merely nip at the fly becomes more common—possibly because the fish are focused on their need to reach the spawning beds.

Irritation

There is much to be said for perseverance when a salmon has risen to your fly without taking. Casting repeatedly over the same fish with a variety of flies—or, more effective, with the same fly at different angles to the current—often results in the fish's finally taking.

The question arises: Is success due to fly choice, presentation, or is it simply a matter of the salmon's becoming irritated enough to take any fly presented at that juncture? I suspect the latter, but there is no unequivocal answer. Repeated casts over an uninterested fish, even with the same fly and with no attempt to change either its speed or presentation, sometimes evokes a solid take.

The angler who encounters a reluctant fish can be in for a long and sometimes frustrating session requiring a variety of flies and approaches. Why spend so much time with one fish? First, there is much satisfaction in taking a difficult fish. To many salmon anglers, locating fish and catching difficult fish are the essence of the sport. When you encounter one reluctant fish, you will certainly run into more, at least for a day or so. What you learn from one difficult salmon will often prove valuable in dealing with others. If you find two reluctant fish in the same pool, alternate between them. As I pointed out in Chapter 4, the positive response of a reluctant fish to a new fly is more likely due to the time interval required to change flies than it is to the new pattern. So the resting periods you create by alternating between two fish in a pool (which may be as long as 10 minutes in a large pool) can work to your advantage.

I remember watching an angler on Quebec's Matane River casting a dry fly to a salmon visibly lying just below a bar. He put cast after cast to various positions around the fish—none of which produced any response. The angler told me he had been casting over the fish for more than an hour. I took up a position below him and began casting to a fish that had rolled there. This kept me busy for at least an hour. An occasional glance upstream confirmed that my neighbor hadn't yet succeeded in bringing his fish up. I finally gave up on my fish, and was wading ashore when I heard a splash. The angler had hooked the salmon after more than two hours of casting to it. Perhaps it is dangerous to assign motives to fish, but it doesn't seem unreasonable that this salmon had finally attacked the fly out of irritation.

Persistent casting can be overdone, however. By the 1980s, the Matane was grossly overfished, its major pools covered by hordes of anglers from dawn to dark. The fish were bombarded with flies almost continuously. Under these circumstances they would not strike, but eventually would leave their lie with a jump and swim wildly about the pool.

Playfulness

A playful response by a salmon is most obvious to a dry fly. Typically, the fish rises with its mouth closed and pushes the fly with its nose. The fish may swirl at the fly or bat it with its tail. Sometimes, changing your fly will bring a serious rise. If it doesn't, it's best to rest the fish and return after an hour or so. If you are lucky, it will rise to your dry fly on the first or second cast.

This breakdown of the salmon's taking motives is not altogether convincing, and is of little use in determining which fly to use. For example, one might assume feeding habit would dictate that a fly pattern be suggestive either of the natural flies active on the river, or of one of the salmon's saltwater prey. This may be the case, but I have never seen such a correlation, nor have I heard of anyone who has. Indeed, with few exceptions (such as Drury's General Practitioner) nearly all salmon wet flies are attractors. The best we can do is to assume, as we start out in the morning, that a good number of fish have entered our pool overnight, or have chosen not to leave it. If we are correct, our success will depend on how well we present the proper fly to them. The crux of the game is to choose a fly that experience tells us has the best chance of success under existing conditions, and to present that fly to a willing fish in an attractive manner. It is essential you do not frighten the fish in the process, since a frightened salmon will seldom take. To arrive at the proper fly, we must take advantage of a rather uncertain correlation between river conditions and the salmon's fly preferences. To accommodate this uncertainty we must proceed as systematically as possible, while recognizing our inability to control the conditions of our fly-selection experiment.

THE USE OF BRIGHTNESS SEQUENCES IN FLY CHOICE

Lacking any indication of how brightness in a fly affects its taking qualities, it seemed expedient to vary it in as systematic a way as possible to see if we could delineate its effect. By *brightness* I do not mean color; rather, I am talking about luminosity: the *intensity* of light reflected by an object, regardless of its colors. Lacking the means to measure the luminosity of flies quantitatively, I decided to construct a series of flies that, in my judgment, varied in brightness. By fishing them in sequence, I hoped to find a level of luminosity that, under the prevalent sky conditions, was most attractive to the salmon. The results have been promising, and I plan to further refine these flies in the future.

On rainy or overcast days I prefer to start with a very dark fly (lowest luminosity) and follow it with flies of increasing brightness. A typical sequence would be Black Squirrel-Orange Butt, Haggis, Lady Joan, and Orange Colburn (Plate 1). On a sunny day I start with a very bright fly, such as the Mickey Finn, and proceed through the Cosseboom[2] and Oriole to the least-bright fly, the Undertaker (Plate 2).

Let us say that on a cloudy morning you have started to work a dark-to-bright sequence of flies. In mid-sequence, the sun comes out brightly. At one time I would have immediately moved to the bright end of the sequence. However, my subsequent experience suggests it is better to continue with the original plan.

Consider again your choice of fly on an overcast day. A fish looking up will see the fly against the sky's mirror-like background. A black fly will afford the best contrast. A fly of any other color will probably offer less contrast, and therefore will be less visible to the fish. An adage that summarizes this approach says, "Bright sky, bright fly; dark sky, dark fly." In my experience, this is of limited validity, but nevertheless it can be useful.

Consider a particular July morning: the sky is heavily overcast, the water is at normal height with a temperature of 58 degrees F (14.4 degrees C). The pool's flow rate is moderate—just fast enough to move the fly at a speed attractive to the salmon. (Knowing what constitutes ideal fly speed comes with experience. I know of no measurements, but I would estimate it to be about 1½ to 2 miles [2.4 to 3.2 kilometers] per hour.) The water's temperature suggests using a wet fly, and its height suggests a size 8. My first choice would be from among such dark patterns as the Black Squirrel-Orange Butt, the Undertaker, the Haggis, or the Blue Charm. I would choose these flies not entirely because of the overcast, but also because I believe these dark patterns usually are more effective during such stream conditions, regardless of light conditions. (If I were fishing the Matane instead of the Miramichi, I would choose a brighter fly.)

After making sure your leader is free of wind knots and nicks, you tie on my first fly choice, the Black Squirrel-Orange Butt. Test the attachment to be sure the turle knot is properly tied and pulled tight. You begin at the head of the pool. On your first pass down you stand as far back from the water's edge as is practical, knowing that fish newly arrived in the pool may be holding close to shore in the early morning (although later they will move to a lie or proceed upstream). You cast at a 45-degree angle to the current (see Figure 4-1). Decrease the distance you move down the pool between the groups of casts (1, 2, 3; 4, 5, 6, etc.), and make your casts shorter and closer together. The object is to work the pool thoroughly to increase your chances of covering any fish present during this prime fishing time. Watch the fly at all times. If you cannot see it, you sight along your line to where your fly *should* be. Your first pass down the pool gives you perhaps your best chance of taking a fish, so you proceed carefully and deliberately. You want to be sure you do not frighten any salmon, thus making them unavailable to you on succeeding passes. Having reached the tail of the pool without moving a fish, you tie on a Haggis and start again at the head. The reason you switch flies is to see if the addition of a bit more color—in this case, the Haggis' bright yellow beard—will change things.

Known lies are critical points, and on your second pass you break the regular pattern of casts to spend a bit more time on them. Now is the time to fish intensively by making more casts and positioning them closer together. You should try slack-line casts of various lengths so that any salmon on the lie will see your fly approaching at various angles to the current.

The second pass down the pool is no more fruitful than was the first. You try a third pass using a Blue Charm. This fly provides a further increase in brightness than previous choices. The body is still black, but the hackle introduces blue to the scheme. In addition, the gray-squirrel wing is tipped white, with black and gray near the fly's head. Moreover, you have gone to an extreme in size by selecting a low-water version of the fly—the equivalent of a size-14 fly tied on a number-8 hook. You haven't enough flies to vary pattern selection in a totally systematic manner. Even if you did, you wouldn't have room to carry them all in your vest, nor the time to present them all before river conditions would have changed enough to undermine comparisons to your earlier passes. But you are being as systematic as you can in a situation where complete control of your fly-choice experiment is impossible.

When a fish comes to the Blue Charm with a swirl, you feel nothing; apparently it was not pricked by the hook. Therefore you did not pull the fly, which could possibly have disturbed the surface enough to frighten him, ruining any chance of bringing him back. You are at position A in Figure 7-2. Your cast landed at position B, and the fish swirled at your Blue Charm when it had reached position C. You sight along line AC and note a distinctive light-colored rock at position D. Sighting back to shore, you note a lone birch at point E. Estimate the distance from position A to the shore so you can walk along line DE and regain position A at some later time. Meanwhile, you have held on to the fly line so you can recast the same length of line (AB) that moved the fish. There is no need to rush this, however. The salmon must first return to its position. It will not lose interest while waiting for the fly to reappear. Quite the contrary: The delay builds up tension in the fish, and could make its next approach much more vigorous. During each fly change you have checked your leader for wind knots, and you now take a look at your Blue Charm to be sure you haven't mashed the hook point with a low back cast. (This could explain your failure to hook the fish that had shown interest—a broken hook may have slid out of its mouth.) But the point is fine, so you proceed, duplicating the previous cast as nearly as possible. It fails to bring the fish up this time, as do a number of other casts wherein you change the line speed as well as the angle of the fly to the current. You wind your fly line to the point where you were holding it when the fish rose. This will allow you to cast exactly the same length of line after you replace the Blue Charm with a size-10 Undertaker.

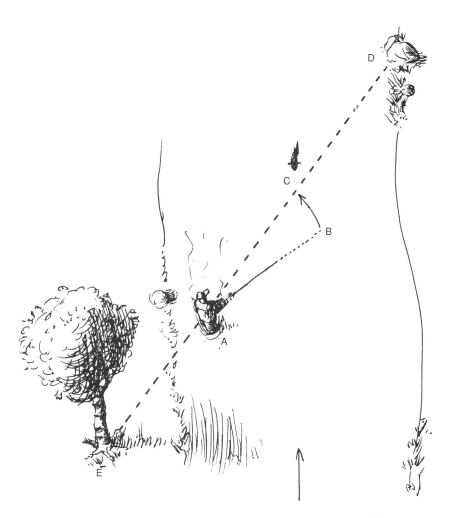

FIGURE 7-2. *Regaining a river position where a fish has been located.*

In such a situation, you are following time-honored advice to change to a smaller fly and, if that doesn't work, a different pattern. However, I don't believe either of these changes is very effective in itself, but they can work because they take enough time to allow more tension to build in the fish. You choose the Undertaker because you have had good luck with it for the last several days (the confidence factor).

On your first cast with the Undertaker, the fly is taken solidly in the same spot where the fish rose originally.

This episode emphasizes a number of practices that increase your probability of taking a fish as opposed to a complete chuck-and-chance-it approach:

- The overcast was factored into choosing the brightness (low) for the class of flies initially presented.
- The water's height, speed, and temperature were factored into the decisions on fly type (wet), size (8), and silhouette (sparse).
- The chosen flies were among those in which the angler had the greatest confidence.
- Watching the fly closely during its swing ensured that a swirl by an interested fish did not go unnoticed.
- Casts were repeatedly made as close as possible to the location where the fish was raised. They were delayed to build tension in the fish, thus making a good take more likely.
- The angle at which the fly approached the salmon's location was varied to find the one most attractive to the fish.
- A fly with which the angler had had recent success was used with good results.
- Fly changes were made as systematically as possible.

Let's not be too impressed with how well things ended this time. It is possible that a bright fly would have worked as well, or even better, on this particular day. On another occasion the size-10 Undertaker might have been useless. However, we probably gave ourselves the best chance by proceeding as we did. If we did make some poor decisions, we will never know about them, since the conditions, the location, and the mood of the fish will not be duplicated in the foreseeable future.

The aforementioned fly sequence is one example of many that could have been devised to meet those specific river conditions. On a bright day I advise you start with a bright fly and work toward the dark ones (Plate 2). With a few years' experience you will have developed a group of flies in which you have confidence. Naturally, you will favor these flies in your brightness sequences, emphasizing those that have proven particularly useful on the river you are presently fishing.

Imagine again you are fishing down the same pool where you caught the salmon. It is 4:00 P.M. of the same day. The sun has been shining brightly since noon, and the water has warmed to 62 degrees F (16.6 degrees C). In light of its success that morning, and despite sequence considerations, you have continued to use the size-10 Undertaker. However, in retying it to your leader you notice that you have been using a 10-pound-test (4.5 kilograms) tippet, which is too large for this small fly. You should have tied on a length of 8-pound test (3.6 kilograms) when you first put it on this morning, and you do so now. You may even decide to extend your leader with a section of 6-pound test (2.7 kilograms) to be sure this small fly will show lifelike mobility in the water.

Suddenly a fish of about 10 pounds (4.5 kilograms) leaps behind you, in water you covered 10 minutes ago. You turn at the sound of the splash and there is no question as to where it is located. Should you retrace your steps and fish down over the spot? You know that a jump doesn't usually indicate a taking fish. On the other hand, you know where a fish is located—at least momentarily—and this is something you should not ignore. If the sky had remained overcast—particularly if the water had been moderately high, making it likely that the fish was running—the probable answer would be no. By the time you got ashore, and got into a position to cover the salmon, it likely would have left the pool. But the conditions now do not favor running, and the fish has jumped close to a known lie. So you get well above the splash, and fish down toward its position. You carefully present the Undertaker, anticipating the fish may come up for it at any minute. But nothing happens, so you change to a size-8 Rusty Rat. The reason here is that the orange of the rear half of the Rat's body may reinforce the fish's attraction to the peacock herl of the Undertaker's dressing, as well as increase the pattern's overall brightness. (Both the Undertaker and the Rusty Rat have peacock herl in their bodies. For the Rusty Rat (Plate 2), the rear half is orange floss.) In addition, you have introduced a black-and-white wing of gray-fox guard hairs, a hallmark of the Rat series.

Either the salmon has moved on, or it is sick of looking at Rusty Rats, because it doesn't respond to your efforts. You now show the fish a size-10 Shady Lady. It likes this no better. You had hoped the fish would be intrigued by the fly's unusual shape, and by its ability to move in or just below the surface film. Not so today.

You give yourself one more chance. You tie on a size-6 Butterfly[3] (Plate 2) and cast it several times over the fish's position. You are testing the possibility that the fish, for whatever reason, wants a larger fly. As the fly swims across the pool toward its target, you give it a series of short jerks to make the splayed wings undulate. When this fails to arouse the fish, you suspect it has indeed moved on. In presenting each of these flies you have varied their angle of approach—but all your strategies have failed.

You take a reading of the river's temperature—64 degrees F (17.7 C)—and wade ashore. The 6-degree F rise since 8:30 A.M. suggests a dry fly might work. You tie on an orange-hackled White Bomber and work the lie where the fish had jumped. After a dozen casts, the fish comes up and bumps your fly with its nose. So, you think, it hasn't left the pool after all; or maybe it has, and has been replaced by another fish. At any rate, you just haven't come up with what this fish wants.

A dozen more casts and the fish bumps again. You then allow the Bomber to drag over the fish's position. The fish comes up and chases it, but then turns away at the last moment.

You replace the White Bomber with one of natural deer hair and having a brown hackle. A dozen casts elicit no action. You cast again, and as the Bomber starts its float, you sporadically move it an inch or so by raising your rod tip. This brings the salmon up with its mouth open wide to engulf your fly. You resist your reaction to pull, waiting until the fish turns down, its tail moving toward the surface, before you set the hook. Your timing is good and you have a good hold on your salmon.

Salient points:

- Do not go back after a fish that jumps in an area you have already covered unless you are reasonably sure it is on a lie and is not running.
- If a fish does not respond to a wet fly during a period when the water temperature is rising, try it with a dry fly.
- Respond to a playful fish by switching to a darker fly. If this doesn't work, try skittering a dry fly.
- Resist the temptation to set immediately on a fish that comes to your dry fly with a great rush. Do not pull too soon or you will pull the fly out of its mouth. But do not wait too long or it will spit out your offering.
- Be willing to spend a considerable amount of time on a fish that comes to your fly without taking. Although such fickleness can be irritating, you probably stand a better chance of taking this fish than you do of finding another in the pool in a taking mood.
- Remember that you don't lose anything by interrupting your fishing to look at your natural surroundings. It may even give you an advantage. After all, the average salmon river is a relatively undisturbed natural scene filled with many interesting plants and animals. Just don't be birdwatching the same time you are fishing.

Imagine that on another occasion you approach a pool you have never fished before. The water temperature is 66 degrees F (18.8 degrees C), which suggests you use a dry fly. But this is a large pool having only a few locations that look promising. You tie on a Green Machine (a green version of the Buck Bug—see Plate 1) and apply flotant. Starting at the head of the pool, you cast across, allowing the fly first to float until the slack is taken up, and then to drag across the current until it is below you. Suddenly, a nice grilse takes your fly up in the heavy water at the head. It's a lively one, and it makes some nice jumps before you pick it up and tag it for the evening's meal.

Moving slowly down the pool, you continue to make the same casts. You cover the promising spots with special care and multiple casts. You do not hesitate to cover the heavy water, as you know there may be lies there not obvious from the surface. A salmon chases the Green Machine while it is dragging, but it turns back and will not come again to this fly, nor to several other Buck Bugs you put over it. After carefully marking the fish's position, you move on.

You are getting close to the tail of the pool. You begin covering an area where the pool is thinning out and the current is picking up speed as it moves toward the lip. A grilse takes your Green Machine, giving you plenty of action before you subdue and release it. Additional casts to the same area with the same fly produce nothing, but you have a feeling there is a salmon in the vicinity. There is no rational basis for this belief, but it's amazing how often these suspicions prove accurate.

You tie on a large White Bomber and cover the area methodically. A salmon comes up out of the heavier water you have already covered and swipes your leader with its tail. Repeat casts prove fruitless. You change to a White Wulff (Plate 3), and after several casts a salmon takes it.

The next day you fish the pool with a little more confidence. You carefully cover the area where you raised a fish, but could not tempt it, with a Green Machine the day before. Lining up your sight marks on both banks, you wade out on the imaginary line between them, fishing short, and then long, with an Oriole. This time you succeed in hooking a good fish.

Things to remember from this experience:

- A Buck Bug is a good fly to explore a pool when conditions indicate you should use a dry fly. The Buck Bug covers water efficiently, having the attraction of a dry fly during the float and the appeal of a commotion fly while dragging. If the water is cool, I usually use a wet fly to explore. However, sometimes a dry fly will work. During the end of one season on the

Miramichi River, when the water temperature was in the high 40s F (around 9 degrees C), I came upon a pool I had never fished before. It was large and featureless. One pass down the pool with a size-4 Mickey Finn produced no response, so I tied on a large Green Machine and went down through it again. I'd had high hopes for the Mickey Finn, and when it didn't produce I made a choice that even at the time seemed a bit bizarre. The Green Machine proved not so strange a choice, however, when a good-sized salmon grabbed it as it dragged across the current.

- Fish will sometimes hold in the fast water at the head of a pool located at the end of a long rapid. They are likely taking advantage of the oxygen-rich water prevalent there. Grilse in particular like to get right up in the heavy flow.
- A large White Bomber is a good dry exploration fly, and is good for raising fish from considerable depths. If the salmon will play with such a fly, you will know their location, and sometimes they will then take a more conventional dry fly.
- Always mark (or better yet, memorize) any location where you raise a fish but cannot get it to take. Once, as I was fishing down a strange pool on the Matane, I came upon a rock that was balanced atop another only a few feet from the water's edge. It dawned on me that this had been done not by the river current, but by another angler. I looked over the water, but could see nothing suggesting a lie. However, a half-dozen casts brought up a good fish. This spot has given up fish on subsequent occasions as well.
- Memorize the locations where you encounter fish in a strange pool. Chances are you have found one of its lies.

Fish are showing in the pool, yet you run through your entire sequence of wet flies with absolutely no response. You try a dry fly, a commotion fly, and a hitched fly. All are completely ignored. You could retire to camp and hope for a better day tomorrow, but you have only a short time left on the river and you want to make it count. In this situation, try to intrigue the salmon you know are present in the pool by showing them something unusual:

- Show them a fly whose size is totally inconsistent with the water conditions. Even though the river is low, tie on a size-4, size-2, or even a larger fly.
- Show them a fly they have never seen, or one they see rarely, such as a fly with spey hackle (Bates, 1970), an experimental fly, or some obscure pattern that once caught your eye, but that you have never used.

Will such things work? Not always (remember that *always* is a bad word for salmon anglers), but they will work often enough to be worth your while.

THE ROLE OF FLY COLOR

Color undoubtedly plays an important role in the salmon's decision whether to take a fly. For every river there seems to be a specific color that works better than others, as Kelson (1895) pointed out. For example, salmon flies emphasizing the color blue are not particularly effective on many rivers, though they are said to be the preferred patterns on Icelandic streams (Jorgenson, 1978) and on Nova Scotia's Margaree. Some anglers speculate this is due to differences in bottom color.

Traditional trout streamers such as the Gray Ghost, the Black Ghost, the Cardinelle, the Herb Johnson Special, the Magog Smelt, and the Mickey Finn occupy a special niche in the salmon angler's arsenal. Dressed on 3XL hooks in sizes 6 through 2, streamers are most useful in the fall, when the salmon seem to prefer big, bright flies. During the spring and summer they are used during periods of high water, and also at normal water levels as change-of-pace flies to stir reluctant fish into action. The bright, colorful members of the genre are used on black salmon, but that fishery has produced a number of specialized streamers as well, such as the Renous Special, the Golden Eagle, and the Rose of New England. These are usually tied on 2/0 single salmon hooks.

The Mickey Finn is such a standout streamer pattern that it is widely used throughout the season tied as a traditional wet salmon fly on size-4 through -8 hooks.

An incident on the Matane illustrates the taking qualities of this fly. Having found the village pool in St. René unoccupied, I proceeded to its tail to start my evening's fishing. It's a relatively small pool, but it has several good lies that had often been productive for me in the past. I had hardly begun when I noticed another angler working the fast water at the head. Presently a loud splash told me he had a fish on and that I had better give him room. Having tired the fish, he tried to set up his tailer (see Chapter 8) with one hand while controlling the fish with the other, but the salmon ran as he was about to cock it. Finally he threw the tailer in my direction and asked me to do the honors. To show his appreciation for having tailed his fish, the angler gave me his place at the head of the pool.

Presently there was another splash. I reeled up and went straight for the tailer, and we soon had his second salmon on the bank. As he now had his daily limit of three fish, he cut off his fly, a poorly tied and badly chewed Mickey Finn, and presented it to me. It had taken all three salmon. I tied it on and fished the rest of the evening without a touch. But the Mickey Finn is now a fly in which I have confidence, and on subsequent occasions it has served me well.

Some anglers argue that differences in water color influence the salmon's color preference. Although many rivers are tinged reddish or brownish from bog runoff, a good many gin-clear rivers hold fish that exhibit color preferences.

In an article in the *Atlantic Salmon Journal* (Autumn 1986), Art Lee suggested that the greater the contrast of a fly's colors with the color of the sky at the time it is being fished, the more attractive it will be to the salmon (or at least when the fish are not taking well). Eric Taverner had alluded to this in his book *Salmon Fishing*, but he did not develop the idea as thoroughly. For example, Taverner noted that, for a time, the salmon of the Lochy River could be risen only by a canary-colored fly during a certain period of the season; during the next season, however, the fly was generally ignored. Taverner ascribed this to a change in the color of the river's water. Of another river in the northwest Scottish Highlands, the Carron, he wrote that "Green Highlander [Plate 4] has long been a favourite and local men demand some green in the patterns they employ."

To judge their suitability, Art Lee views salmon flies against the sky before tying them on. This is, of course, the same way salmon look at them. Lee says a fly that "jumps out" at you when you view it this way will be more effective than those that do not—but only if the salmon are not taking well. This, he claims, explains why the effectiveness of a salmon fly will vary from season to season, day to day, or hour to hour.

Since his article appeared, I have had many opportunities to test Art Lee's theory. I must say, while it does not answer all the problems of fly selection, it works better than pure chance. My problem with it is this: As often as not, two flies showing little difference in their contrast with the sky will show pronounced differences in effectiveness. In certain light it is very difficult to find any fly that will "jump" out at you. By running sequences, you can overcome such problems and also accommodate other factors in the salmon's taking decision.

The LaFontaine Color Theory

This was about all anyone knew of the influence of color in salmon flies until, in 1990, Gary LaFontaine published his book *The Dry Fly: New Angles*,

Recipes for Plate 1

1. COLONEL MONELL

Tail: Five or six whisks of hackle
Body: Peacock herl
Ribbing: Red floss
Hackle: Gray Plymouth Rock cock, palmered
Type: Dry

2. BOMBER

(See Chapter 6, page 88)
Type: Dry/commotion

3. GREEN MACHINE

Hook: Mustad 3399A, 4, 6, 8
Tag: Fluorescent green wool
Tail: Green bucktail
Body: Green deer hair spun and trimmed to a
  cigar shape
Hackle: Brown, palmered over the body
Type: Dry/commotion

4. BLACK SQUIRREL-ORANGE BUTT

Tag: Oval silver tinsel
Tip: Fluorescent orange floss
Tail: Black hackle fibers
Ribbing: Oval silver tinsel
Body: Black wool
Throat: Black hackle
Wing: Black squirrel tail
Type: Wet

5. HAGGIS

Tag: Silver tinsel
Tip: None
Tail: None
Ribbing: Oval silver tinsel
Body: Black floss
Throat: Mixture of fibers from a yellow saddle
  hackle with a few soft fibers from the base of
  the feather
Wing: Black bear hair
Type: Wet

6. LADY JOAN

Tag: Oval gold tinsel
Tip: None
Tail: None
Ribbing: Oval gold tinsel
Body: Orange Floss
Throat: Fibers from a yellow saddle hackle
  with a few soft fibers from the base of the
  feather
Wing: Gray squirrel tail over black bear hair
Type: Wet

7. ORANGE COLBURN

Tag: Oval silver tinsel
Tip: None
Tail: Orange hackle fibers
Ribbing: None
Body: Fluorescent orange floss with a butt
  of black ostrich herl in the center
Throat: Orange hackle, collar style
Wing: Orange dyed gray squirrel
Type: Wet

Plate I

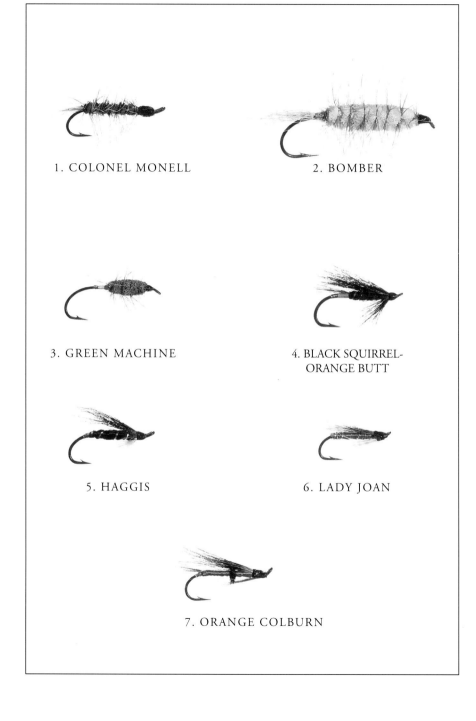

1. COLONEL MONELL

2. BOMBER

3. GREEN MACHINE

4. BLACK SQUIRREL-
ORANGE BUTT

5. HAGGIS

6. LADY JOAN

7. ORANGE COLBURN

PLATE 2

8. MICKEY FINN

9. COSSEBOOM

10. ORIOLE

11. UNDERTAKER

12. RUSTY RAT

13. SHADY LADY

14. BUTTERFLY

Recipes for Plate 2

8. MICKEY FINN

Tag: None
Tip: None
Tail: None
Ribbing: None
Body: Flat silver tinsel
Throat: None
Wing: Yellow bucktail with sparse side
  strips of red bucktail
Type: Wet

9. COSSEBOOM

Tag: Embossed silver tinsel
Tip: None
Tail: Green floss
Ribbing: Embossed silver tinsel
Body: Green floss
Throat: Yellow hackle, collar style
Wing: Gray squirrel tail
Type: Wet

10. ORIOLE

Tag: Oval gold tinsel
Tail: Fibers from a red golden pheasant body
  feather
Ribbing: Oval gold tinsel
Body: Black wool or floss*
Throat: Brown hackle
Wing: Mallard flank dyed green drake
Type: Wet
*A peacock herl body is a valuable variation

11. UNDERTAKER

Tag: Flat gold tinsel
Tips: Rear—fluorescent green floss; Front—
  fluorescent orange floss
Tail: None
Ribbing: Oval gold tinsel
Body: Peacock herl
Throat: Black hackle
Wing: Black bear hair
Type: Wet

12. RUSTY RAT

Tag: Oval gold tinsel
Tail: Peacock sword fibers
Ribbing: Oval gold tinsel
Body: Rear—fluorescent orange floss;
  Front—bronze peacock herl
Wing: Guard hair from a gray fox
Hackle: Grizzly, collar style
Head: Red
Type: Wet

13. SHADY LADY

Tip: Fluorescent orange floss
Body: Peacock herl
Body hackle: Brown, dry-fly quality
Type: Wet

14. BUTTERFLY

Tail: Red dyed hackle fibers
Body: Peacock herl
Wing: White calf body hair tied split to give
  a V and at a 45-degree slope to the shank
Hackle: Brown, dry-fly quality
Type: Wet

15. GREEN MACHINE PHOTOGRAPHED IN GREEN LIGHT

(See Plate 1)

16. FULKRO

Tag: Oval silver tinsel
Tip: Fluorescent orange floss
Tail: Red dyed calf tail
Ribbing: Oval silver tinsel
Body: Black wool
Throat: Brown hackle
Wing: Red squirrel tail
Type: Wet

17. SILVER RAT

Tag: Oval gold tinsel
Ribbing: Oval gold tinsel
Body: Flat silver tinsel
Throat: Grizzly hackle, collar style
Wing: Gray fox guard hair
Type: Wet

18. WHITE WULFF

Tail: White bucktail
Body: Cream-colored wool
Wing: White bucktail
Hackle: Brown saddle
Type: Dry

19. RAT-FACED MACDOUGAL

Tail: Ginger fibers
Body: Clipped light ginger deer hair
Wing: White calf hair
Hackle: Ginger
Type: Dry

PLATE 3

15. GREEN MACHINE
*Photographed in
Green Light*

16. FULKRO

17. SILVER RAT

18. WHITE WULFF

19. RAT-FACED
MACDOUGAL

PLATE 4

20. WHISKERS

21. ROYAL WULFF

22. MACINTOSH

23. GREEN
HIGHLANDER

24. THE PRIEST

25. THE SILVER &
BLACK

20. WHISKERS

Tail: Gray squirrel hair
Body: Green yarn palmered with brown
    hackle
Wing: Deer body hair pulled in a semicircle
    and tilted a bit forward
Type: Dry/commotion

21. ROYAL WULFF

Tail: White bucktail
Body: Scarlet wool with peacock butts fore
    and aft
Wings: White bucktail
Hackle: Two brown saddles
Type: Dry

22. MACINTOSH

Body: Floss in your favorite color, but sparse
Wing: Gray squirrel tail tied in caddis style at
    midhook
Hackle: Two brown saddles
Type: Dry

23. GREEN HIGHLANDER

Tag: Oval silver tinsel
Butt: Black ostrich tail
Tail: Golden pheasant crest
Ribbing: Oval silver tinsel
Body: Rear quarter, golden yellow floss;
    remainder, bright green floss
Body Hackle: Green
Throat: Lemon hackle
Wing: Red squirrel tail over two strands each
    of yellow and green fluorescent floss over
    sparse orange dyed gray squirrel tail
Type: Wet

24. THE PRIEST

Tag: Oval silver tinsel
Tail: Light blue dun hackle fibers
Ribbing: Oval silver tinsel
Body: Fluorescent white wool
Wing: White calf tail
Throat: Light blue dun, collar style
Type: Wet

25. THE SILVER & BLACK

Tag: None
Tip: None
Tail: None
Ribbing: None
Body: Flat silver tinsel
Throat: Black hen hackle
Wing: Black squirrel tail
Type: Wet

in which he develops a convincing theory of how color can influence the taking decision of trout contemplating attractor-type dry flies. LaFontaine goes
on to speculate, "Could someone work out a Theory of Attraction for underwater flies? Probably not for dead-drift methods. The difficulty of the task is
reflected in the fact that almost all nymph patterns are imitations, general or specific (seen any red-and-white artificial nymphs around?)."

Of course we have not, but I have seen many hundreds of wet Atlantic
salmon flies tied in all colors of the rainbow. They are almost certainly attractors,
since the salmon does not feed on its spawning run, and shows no preference for
patterns that might conceivably suggest naturals present in the river.

The Atlantic salmon and the brown trout have a common ancestor (both are
of the genus *Salmo*), which could argue that they have basically the same feeding habits, the salmon's modified by its anadromous lifestyle. Indeed, many
salmon have been caught with wet trout flies, particularly those featuring
brighter colors. You'll recall that Father Smith tied the first Bomber, one of the
most successful salmon dry flies, after watching a boy catch a large sea-run
brown trout with a spun-deer-hair mouse. In this case, at least, the two fish seem
to react similarly to flies.

In essence, LaFontaine's color theory says that the more intense the color of
an attractor fly, the better it attracts trout. But, he adds, the color in a fly reacts
to the light in which it is viewed. To quote LaFontaine's example: "Pour reddish light on a green fly and it's still green, but a very dull green. The complementary color in the incident light dulls. Pour greenish light on a red fly and
it's still red but not so intense." However, by pouring green light on a green fly,
or red light on a red fly, we can add to their color intensity or, as LaFontaine puts
it, render them "on fire" (Art Lee's "jumps out"?). In doing so, we add to their
attraction. To my mind, this is a more explicit statement of Art Lee's observations, and of the similar concepts mentioned by Eric Taverner as they apply to
wet salmon flies. Let me emphasize that these are not random speculations by
LaFontaine; rather, they have been extensively tested by his group with underwater observations of the trout's reactions to dry attractor flies.

One of the most successful flies in the history of salmon fishing is the
Butterfly. It is nothing more than a Royal Coachman tied with the so-called
bat wings. Of the Royal Coachman, LaFontaine writes:

*No one has been able to explain why it catches so many trout, but empirical
success has made it (especially in the forms of the Royal Wulff and the Royal Trude)*

the most popular color combination for a fly in our country .

The doubters dislike it because it's such a bright fly—but they are wrong. It is not bright. It is half-bright. Under most light conditions the Royal Coachman is a fly possessing both dull and bright materials. When the red floss and the coachman brown hackle and tail (which have red accents) are bright under a red-orange light, the green is dull; when the green peacock herl (a vibrant lively material) is bright under a green light, the red is dull.

This explains the effectiveness of the Royal Coachman. It is not a garish dandy floating down a river. It is a rough simulation of an insect, either a mayfly in upwing variations or caddis fly in downwing variations, that has touches of brightness that focus attention and attract trout. As well as any fly, it stretches reality without breaking it in most situations on trout streams.

Besides exemplifying the LaFontaine Theory of Color Attraction, this quotation suggests to me that the theory applies to wet salmon flies as well as dry trout flies. The Butterfly's outstanding record now makes sense. Anglers interested in solving the problem of salmon-fly selection for various situations should familiarize themselves with LaFontaine's theory and see if they can put it to work on the salmon rivers. If the theory proves inapplicable, very little will have been lost as compared to using a purely hit-or-miss approach to salmon fly color decisions as most of us do now.

There are times when fish will show a pronounced preference for a particular color in wet flies—more often than not, a preference for green. If salmon are in a green-taking mood they will be easier to catch using such flies as the Cosseboom, the Colburn Special, the La Verte, the Green Butterfly, the Green Machine, or the Green Highlander.

The leaves of trees are green because their chlorophyll absorbs all colors in the spectrum *except* green. Thus, light filtered through leaves should be effective in setting green flies "afire." Based on this, we can speculate that the fish's increased attraction to green flies is due to green-rich light setting them "afire." LaFontaine notes: "Even if there is no hatch to match, the trout on tree-lined streams respond better to predominantly green flies . . . For years this was a mystery to me—now it is not. Green is the most important color of attraction. Except for particular seasons—such as very early spring before the trees bud— or autumn when the leaves change, or on open rivers where trees don't tower over, or even cover, the water—green is the most effective choice."

It strikes me that on large rivers, where little of the waters can be shaded by trees, green enhancement would be most pronounced when the sun was low in the sky (Figure 7-3). Only then would light pass through the treetops and, with its green component intensified, strike the river. It would follow that these effects should be greatly diminished during an overcast. Unfortunately, my fishing diaries are insufficiently detailed for me to speak one way or the other.

Others might say that the salmon, seeing good numbers of green naturals on the water, takes them into its mouth in response to memories of its parr days, when it feasted on the same hatch. I cannot say I have ever seen a hatch of green flies at the same time the fish were exhibiting a preference for green artificials, although such hatches are common. Nor have I found green flies in the

FIGURE 7-3. *Light from low sun green-intensified by passage through leaves.*

throat of any fish caught during a hatch of green flies. And not once have I taken a fish by changing to a green pattern in response to a hatch of green naturals. So as far as I'm concerned, the hatch-matching theory is virtually worthless. However, the brightness-sequence approach (bright-to-dark or dark-to-bright sequences) will give you the opportunity to pick up a fish in a green-taking mood if some of the flies in the sequence have green components.

The color of relatively minor fly components, such as the head, butt, or tail, can be decisive on occasion. Traditionally, the Rat series of flies are tied with a red head, but some anglers feel a black one works better on certain rivers. Salmon-fishing literature is filled with opinion. Some writers claim that flies tied with a red head are superior to the same patterns dressed with black ones; others say head color is unimportant. For what it's worth, my own experience has taught me to favor flies with red heads.

There is also a good deal of divergent opinion on the best color for the butts of flies, such as those in the Black Bear series.[4] Whether red, orange, yellow, or green is best is the subject of endless discussion, though salmon anglers generally agree that fluorescent colors work best. A few patterns have two butts. The Undertaker has two butts as well as a tag, which perhaps offer a better chance that the fish's preferred color is present.

Red—The Neglected Color

In their book *Hair-Wing Atlantic Salmon Flies*, Keith Fulsher and Charles Krom wrote of a fly called the Fulkro (Plate 3). It had a wing of gray squirrel and was distinguished by a tail of red-dyed calf, which they say showed up very well in the water. This fly produced well over a period of four days on the Miramichi when nothing else seemed to work and no other anglers were taking fish. The Fulkro, the authors note, has "produced fish since, but never with the initial regularity." I would be interested to know whether the Fulkro might be more productive if fished later in the season, during the red-rich light of autumn. Regardless, I believe minor color variations, whether in the tail or at the head, have real effects on the taking quality of a fly, and can perhaps be explained by LaFontaine's ideas on the effects of incident light.

Salmon take orange flies better in the fall than they do at other times of the year. LaFontaine affirms this is also true for trout. Orange flies, he points out, have always been favorites for autumn steelhead (another member of the genus *Salmo*). "The orange leaves," he writes, "are the major reason that an orange attractor is so successful—even to the point where it is an all-day dry fly if nothing is hatching. On heavily wooded canopy rivers, orange leaves are not only along side and above the water, but they are floating on it when they fall."

In 1935, Preston Jennings penned the first American work dealing with entomology for anglers: *A Book of Trout Flies*. In it, he states his belief that fish perceive the color red more intensely than do human beings[5], and uses this to explain the greater taking reaction to red flies. Jennings' conclusions may find support if we consider the red tail of the Fulkro fly and the traditional red head of the Rat series and the Cosseboom. However, in a large sampling of salmon flies, red is not a particularly popular color. Of the 276 patterns listed in Fulsher and Krom's *Hair-Wing Atlantic Salmon Flies*, only 28 percent have any red in their composition; of those a mere 12 percent feature it as a major component, such as a wing or body. We can speculate that in our world of green vegetation, the red components of flies are muted because they are so often viewed with green-intensified light (its complementary color).

PATIENCE IS NECESSARY

Sometimes the search for the taking fly is long. I recall a fish on the Matane that kept me occupied for close to two hours. It announced itself by swirling at my Silver Rat. Several more casts with the same fly went ignored. During the next hour I ran through a succession of wet flies, none of which interested the fish. I knew it was still on its lie, for it came up to push my White Wulff with its nose. Repeated casts with the Wulff brought no further response. I tied on a succession of dry patterns, including a Rat-Faced MacDougall, a Whiskers, and a Royal Wulff (Plate 4)—none of which tempted it. Next I showed it a MacIntosh, and the salmon attempted to drown it with his tail. I went back to the fly that had originally moved the fish, the Silver Rat (Plate 3). This time it was not interested. But when I switched to a Green Highlander, the fish took the fly with great gusto. You may ask why the Green Highlander was ultimately successful. Had the fish been waiting for two hours for me to show it a green fly? Or was it irritated with the number of flies that had passed over and finally attacked one in anger? I haven't the faintest idea, since I am not at all sure whether fish have such thought processes. You might well ask why I didn't show him the Green Highlander after the aborted rise to the Silver Rat. At that point, I had a good deal more confidence in the other wets. In reflection, I am tempted to think that the Highlander was the only offering that was "afire."

Of course, the ultimate frustration of the salmon angler is to fish the river for several days during a sparse run without success. To improve the lot of the salmon and ensure its survival, all salmon anglers must join the battle and support the Atlantic Salmon Federation and any of the various river associations.

NOTES

1. While fishing the Moisie River in 1964, Lee Wulff and some of his friends started the Sixteen/Twenty Club. To become a member you had to land a salmon of 20 pounds (9 kilograms) or more using a fly tied on a size-16 or smaller hook. Lee tied up a new fly, the Prefontaine Skater (named in honor of his host, Alain Prefontaine), having a "snoot of bucktail" to maximize its visibility to the fish. It had to be presented using a 4-pound-test (1.8 kilograms) tippet. Alain Prefontaine became the club's first member by landing a 20-pound, 6-ounce (9.2 kilograms) fish that evening. Lee became the second member a few days later when he landed two 24-pounders (10.9 kilogram), one in 32 minutes and the other in 38.

2. It is said that a girl brought John Cosseboom his lunch to eat on the bank of a salmon river he was fishing. Cosseboom was so taken with the yellow sweater she was wearing, that that evening he tied a fly with bright-yellow hackle—the fly now bearing his name.

3. The Butterfly was first tied by Maurice Ingalls in 1956. Father Elmer Smith, who knew Ingalls well, told me the Coachman was Ingalls' favorite trout fly in Maine. After being introduced to Atlantic salmon on the Miramichi, Ingalls decided to tie some Coachman flies for salmon fishing. Ingalls adapted the Butterfly's distinctive splayed wings from a bass fly called the Batwing, invented by his casting instructor, Bill Edson.

4. In the early 1920s, Harry Smith developed a fly on Maine's Narraguagus River using bear hair for both the throat and wing. He called it the Black Bear. Later, on the Miramichi, Ira Gruber invented his Gorilla, which had a wing of "darkest woodchuck." He followed this creation with the Spider, which had a wing of black squirrel and an orange butt. The Gruber patterns had black bodies with silver ribbing and black hackle. They were the forerunners of the Black Bear series, which differed from each other mostly in the number of their butts and their color. When they became available, fluorescent materials were preferred.

5. In his book *The Well-Tempered Angler*, Arnold Gingrich tells of fishing for 12 straight hours without catching a trout. After dinner, an elderly gentleman approached him and offered him a dark-red, size-10 nymph, which he thought might change Gingrich's luck that evening. He had serious reservations about using it, though, especially when the donor told him it was the nymph of the Royal Coachman. "It's sort of like the Admiral of the Swiss Navy then," Gingrich remarked. However, out in the

river, he took 12 trout on it within 40 minutes. Now, of course, he was curious as to who the old gentleman was. It was Preston Jennings, who later explained that there was indeed a Royal Coachman natural (*Isonychia bicolor*). He ascribed the potency of the fly to the fact that the darting of the natural nymph was comparable in speed to the retrieve of the average angler. He also believed that its red color was equally important.

CHAPTER 8

Fish On!

*HAL.—He is a large grilse, I see by his play; or
a young salmon, of the earliest born this spring.
Hold him tight; he will fight hard.
PHYS.—There! he springs out of the water!
Once, twice, thrice, four times! He is a merry
one!*

—Sir Humphrey Davy, *Salmonia*

UPON HOOKING A FISH, TROUT ANGLERS OFTEN EXCLAIM "I'VE GOT ONE!" Such is not the case with Atlantic salmon. The battle with this large, powerful fish pits your angling skill and equipment against its survival instincts. Salmon anglers know they haven't "got" anything except a maniac at the end of a thread, and are more likely to announce "Fish on!" as a warning to nearby anglers to give room. (It is an unwritten rule that when an angler near you hooks up, you should leave the water until the fish is under control.)

THE MINUTE-PER-POUND RULE

The rule of thumb is that the fight should take one minute for each pound (0.45 kilogram) the fish weighs. As I see it, however, this rule assumes you are an experienced angler fighting a two-sea-year fish of 8 to 12 pounds (3.6 to 5.4 kilograms), and accounts for no unusual hazards. A grilse often wages a battle that leads you to believe it is a much larger fish. You will be very lucky to land such a fish in five or six minutes, and you'll gain new respect for the grilse as a gamefish. Grilse are much more prone to jumping than are older salmon, and will often perform a series of leaps. They also take a fly better than their elders.

Beginning anglers tend to take longer to land salmon because they are reluctant to fight them hard. Going too easy with a salmon gives it an opportunity to rest, prolonging the fight. After even a brief rest, a salmon will return to battle with almost the same vigor with which it began. As we shall see, beginners also lose fish because they underestimate the hazards involved in landing them.

SETTING THE HOOK

There is usually little doubt when an Atlantic salmon takes your wet fly. When the fish strikes, set the hook immediately by raising the rod tip, giving it a good strong pull to sink it home. There are those who advise you allow the fish to set the hook during the fight. Some even suggest you give the fish line so the hook will slide to one corner of its mouth, a softer area, before setting. By delaying, I feel you risk the fish's rejecting the fly or the fly's simply falling out of the fish's mouth. Remember how hard you could pull on the tippet without breaking it during your experiment? You can pull this hard to set the hook.

PLAYING THE FISH

Taking Up Slack

After you've set the hook you must get the fish on the reel. I once saw an angler hook a good fish only to have the fish immediately run directly toward him. The angler began to strip line, with the current carrying the slack downstream in a big loop. Still running, the salmon swam right through the loop and past the angler. Within moments the loop tightened against the rod and the fish broke off. This angler could have kept his fish by backing away from the charging fish to take up slack (granted, with rocky and slimy river bottoms this is not always possible). Usually you can take up slack as you keep a tight line on the fish by pressing the line against the rod with your index finger. Be prepared to release the pressure if the fish decides to run, in which case you must guide the slack through the first stripping guide so it does not tangle. This can be done by running the line through a circle formed with the thumb and index finger of your line hand—a sort of giant stripping guide. The fish's first run will be as strong as any it will make. Make no attempt to slow it. Point your rod in the fish's direction, but keep the tip up so the rod can absorb any sudden stress the fish might exert.

Your objective now is to tire the fish as quickly as possible. A long fight can severely exhaust or even kill a fish. Going easy on the salmon does it no favors; you must be aggressive and beat it quickly.

Bowing to the Fish

The first run often ends with a leap. You can anticipate this if you see the end of the fly line approaching the surface. If the salmon jumps from the water and falls across a taut leader, its weight could pull the fly out of its mouth. Therefore, when the fish clears the water, lower your rod tip quickly to give instant slack. But as soon as the fish lands, tighten immediately. This is called *bowing to the fish*. Be prepared for a series of closely spaced leaps or wild thrashing at the surface—all of which require a bow.

Keeping Level with the Fish

After its initial wild burst, the fish will hunker down to do battle. As soon as it does, calmly make your way to shore, prepared to stop and deal with the fish if necessary. You want to fight the fish from shore because you want to keep approximately level with it as it moves along the river, and you cannot follow it

STREAM COURTESY

If another angler in your pool hooks a fish, it is incumbent upon you to do everything possible to help him. The first thing you should do is reel up and get out of his way, moving up the bank until the fish is well under control. If you are fishing rotation, you may find a few rods reluctant to move for you. Usually a little good-natured needling from the group will resolve this. On larger pools it may be all right for you to continue fishing while another angler plays his salmon, provided you keep a close eye on the action and are prepared to move if the fish comes your way.

There was a time when it was considered bad manners to fish any closer to another angler than twice the length of a maximum cast. With the great increase in the popularity of fly-fishing in recent years, this rule seems to have gone the way of gut leaders. The spacing between anglers fishing rotation is seldom that great, though I still emphasize this rule to my fly-casting pupils because I think most who violate it do so out of ignorance. I hate to see discourtesy intrude into a sport that was largely free from it when I began.

It's common sense that you should not do anything that would frighten any salmon in the pool. Almost invariably, such transgressions result from the failure to understand just how easy it is to scare a fish, either by walking along the shingle, by casting a shadow over the fish, or by wading noisily. Salmon seldom bolt when frightened; to the uninitiated, this wrongly suggests that the fish is not aware of human presence.

> *O, the gallant fisher's life,*
> *It is the best of any;*
> *'Tis full of pleasure, void of strife,*
> *And't is beloved by many:*
> *Other joys*
> *Are but toys,*
> *Only this*
> *Lawful is;*
> *For our skill*
> *Breeds no ill*
> *But content and pleasure.*

—Jo. Chalkhill, quoted by Izaak Walton in *The Compleat Angler: The Contemplative Man's Recreation.*

fast enough while wading. If the fish gains a position either significantly upstream or downstream from you, the new angle of the hook relative to the fish can cause it to loosen and ultimately pull out.

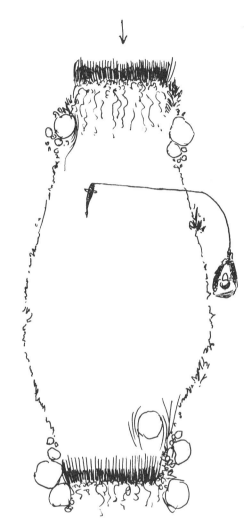

FIGURE 8-1. *When fighting a salmon you want to try to keep approximately level with the fish.*

A salmon often resists you by going to the bottom of the river and swimming with its head down and its body at an angle to the stream bottom. Although this tires the fish somewhat, running and jumping tire it faster. You can break this deadlock by moving below the fish and applying side pressure, holding the rod low and parallel to the water, pulling the fish's head around. Now the fish will

LASSO YOUR FISH

I had hooked a good salmon on the Matane and had him pretty well played out. My companion made ready to net it when it surfaced and began thrashing. I gave the fish some slack. After a minute or so, the fish settled, and when I tightened, it moved off on a short run. When I pumped the rod to move it back toward the waiting net, the fish seemed a good deal stronger, and the rod was throbbing.

I had never experienced this feeling before. At this point my companion informed me the fish was coming in tail first. This made no sense at all—but he was right. After netting the fish, we found the hook was no longer in the fish's mouth, but had formed a noose with the leader around the fish's tail. I have since learned that other anglers have had the same experience.

have to fight both you and the current to hold its position. As soon as the salmon is broadside to the flow it will break into another run. By then you should have your rod tip up again.

Sometimes while at the bottom a fish (usually a male) will shake its head. This is called *chugging*, and it often allows the fish to shake the hook. Use side pressure as well to counter a salmon's chugging.

The Downstream Run

Occasionally a fish will bolt downstream. Besides giving the fish an advantageous angle, a downstream run presents the possibility the fish might leave the pool. This can mean trouble if your downstream shore is cluttered with boulders, logs, or other impediments that make it difficult, if not impossible to follow the fish. You should investigate a strange pool before fishing it, and keep such things in mind even on familiar pools.

Some anglers recommended you give the fish several yards of line if it seems about to run out of the pool. This line will belly downstream behind the fish. The strong current of the rapid below will pull on the belly and, according to the experts, the fish will react to this pressure by turning and swimming upstream. This is because a salmon will almost always swim in the opposite direction from which it is being pulled. A number of writers describe having used this technique successfully. On the few occasions I have tried it, however, the fish

FIGURE 8-2. *A hooked salmon will often head toward the tail of a pool.*

kept right on going downstream, and not being able to follow it, it broke me off in the rapids below the tail of the pool. Your only alternative when a fish heads toward the pool's tail and you cannot follow it down the rapids below is to hold your rod straight above your head, hold on, and hope it will turn before it reaches heavy water. Obviously you should avoid the tail of the pool. If your fish has maneuvered you near there, try walking it up to the head. Holding the rod high, walk slowly upstream, keeping an eye on the fish in case it reacts with a jump. Usually the salmon will follow you like a dog on a leash. There is some chance this maneuver may cause the hook to pull out, but usually the salmon follows docilely unless you try to move it upstream by reeling. For whatever reason, reeling in line while trying to move a salmon upstream excites the fish, and seems to reinforce its determination to leave the pool.

Despite your best efforts, occasionally a hooked fish will leave the pool. With luck you can follow it down along the fast water to fight it in the pool below. Along the way you likely will have to deal with rocks, which can foul your line. When following salmon through a rocky area, keep as short a line as possible. Submerged rocks usually pose little problem unless the fish decides to circle them. Rocks protruding above the surface are trickier, for a hooked salmon encountering a rock in a rapid almost invariably will choose to go outside the rock rather than inside. When this happens you have to get your line over the top of the rock. Hold your rod at arm's length over your head, and hope you get your line high enough to clear the top of the rock. Meanwhile, attempt to keep up with the fish, and avoid tripping over any streamside debris. Sometimes you can use line pressure to persuade a fish to swim to the inside of rock. But this is by no means easy if the fish is well below you.

Your reel's backing is your safety net, as it were, when a fish's run exceeds the length of your fly line. Be stingy with it, however. Don't allow the fish to take any more than is necessary, and palm the reel judiciously to make it work for every inch. After a run, recover backing as soon as possible. A large downstream belly in fast water means you have no idea what your fish is up to, and can do little to control it. The longer your line, the more control the fish has.

Wind recovered backing and line evenly onto the spool. If you allow it to build up on one side, it may fall over and be buried by incoming line. During the next run, this buried line could stop the reel dead, and the fish could break off.

Keeping the Pressure On

Eventually the fish begins to tire. Its runs are less vigorous, and you can move it toward you more easily. This is the time to subdue the fish. Whatever it does, you do the opposite. If it goes left, you exert side pressure to the right. You are now in position to gain line and slowly bring the fish into shallower water. You'll eventually want to land it in a shallow area of minimal current and devoid of large rocks or other obstructions. If you haven't already, take the best available shore position at this time. The beginner often makes the mistake of assuming the battle is won at this point, and attempts to hurry the fish. Know that as soon as the fish realizes it is getting into shallow water it will make a run for the deep. If you are unprepared for this, you may lose your fish. When you bring the salmon into the shallows a second or third time, it will show more and more signs of fatigue, and will begin to roll on its side. Cautiously shorten the line, but be ready to let the fish run if it makes a strong move toward deep water. Each of these episodes will add to the salmon's fatigue. You will find the runs become shorter each time, and the fish's tendency to roll on its side more pronounced. Since you plan to release this fish, you only want to play it for as long as it takes to extract the hook. At this stage—*and not before*—you may want to grasp your rod above the handle to obtain better maneuverability of the fish. Go easy here; exert line pressure only to coax the struggling fish to move itself toward you.

LANDING FISH

Excluding gaffing, which is illegal on many rivers and has no place on a no-kill stream, there are four ways you can land a played-out salmon.

Beaching and Tailing

Some anglers beach their fish, leading it to a gently sloping shore after it is well played out, and lifting its head out of the water as they slowly slide its body up the bank. Do not pull hard; let the fish's flopping about ease its passage. You then grasp the fish firmly at the base of its tail (caudal peduncle). Most anglers object to beaching on the grounds that it too can damage the fish's protective mucus. It is better to *hand-tail* the fish while it's still in the water. First, wade into water of knee depth. To proceed you're going to need both hands free. I usually insert my rod reel-first into my waders. Grip the fish at the base of its tail. There is a knob near there that, when squeezed, calms the fish as if it were anesthetized. While holding the fish in the water, remove the hook with a pair of hemostat pliers. (Do not lock your hemostat pliers on your vest unless they have a nonreflective finish. Otherwise their flash could frighten fish. If you do not want to store them in a vest pocket, lock them onto a safety pin *inside* your vest.) It's best to grasp the hook across the gape just forward of the fly's tail. Before extracting the hook, rotate it sharply in a 90-degree arc to disengage the barb. You can estimate your salmon's weight by measuring its length or, more accurately, my measuring its length and girth. More accurate still is to weight the salmon in a knotless cotton-mesh net (see Appendix C).

Tailing a fish is easier to do with a *mechanical tailer.* This is essentially a noose of heavy spring steel at the end of a handle. Although it is not completely troubleproof, the tailer is a reasonably efficient way to land a fish. Because it damages the fish's tail muscles, however, it is illegal on no kill waters.

Netting

Netting is not the best way to land a salmon you intend to release. A net big enough to handle a large salmon is nothing you want to haul around with you onstream. Neither is it the best way to handle a fish you plan to release if the cords and knots of your net remove the struggling fish's protective mucus.

If you must net a salmon, however, a knotless net of cotton mesh is best. Nevertheless, many guides continue to use the traditional hard, knotted ones because that's what they've used all their lives.

Netting requires teamwork. When the salmon is played out, the guide sinks

FIGURE 8-3. *If you must use a net, nets of knotless cotton mesh are best for landing salmon you intend to release.*

the net in the river and the angler, well up on shore, steers the fish over it. The guide should never chase the salmon, as this will only drive the fish into deeper water. Swooping the net may hit the leader and pull the hook out. You and your guide should agree on the netting location beforehand, during the early stages of the fight. When you finally bring the fish directly over the sunken net, your guide should bring it up smartly.

Reviving the Fish

After you have removed the hook, your responsibility to the fish has not ended. If the fish must be revived, hold it by its tail with your other hand under its belly. Never hold a fish vertically for any more than a few seconds. One Canadian study exercised hatchery-raised trout to exhaustion, then removed them from the water for 60 seconds. Within 12 hours 72 percent of the fish died. A control group that was exercised but not removed from the water had a survival rate of 88 percent (*Atlantic Salmon Journal*, Autumn 1992). All those who hold a fish out of water to take pictures should give this serious thought. It also underscores that we should minimize the length of the fight.

Don't release your hold on the fish's tail immediately. Wait until you're sure it's capable of proceeding without difficulty. A dead salmon, placed in the river to preserve it from the sun's heat, will be quickly consumed by eels. It's possible that an exhausted salmon could be similarly attacked. Hold the fish in a normal swimming position facing into a moderate current so water may move over its gills. Depending on the fight, the fish's recuperation period may last up to ten minutes or more. When it has recovered it will sweep its tail vigorously, at which point you can safely release it.

Never forget that the fish you hold has survived much adversity to get where it is. We are obligated to do everything possible to see that it completes its journey.

CHAPTER 9

Salmon Conservation Past and Future

PHYS.—Do you think the saw-mills hurt the fishing?

HAL.—I do not doubt it. The immense quantity of sawdust which floats in the water, and which forms hills along the banks, must be poisonous to the fish, by sometimes choking their gills and interfering with their respiration.

—Sir Humphrey Davy, *Salmonia*

LONG BEFORE *HOMO SAPIENS* ROSE TO PROMINENCE IN THE ANIMAL kingdom, *Salmo salar* filled the rivers of Europe from Spain and Portugal to the British Isles, throughout the Baltic Sea and northward to Iceland and the Kola peninsula of Russia. In North America it flourished from Connecticut to the Ungava Peninsula in northern Quebec, and ranged as far east as southwestern Greenland. As with so many of the Earth's creatures, the Atlantic salmon has been no match for man. It survives today in Canada, Iceland, Great Britain, Norway, Russia, Finland, Sweden, and in a few rivers in northern Spain. Essentially all of the United States population is found in Maine. Let us look now at the shameful near demise of the Atlantic salmon in North America.

Early European explorers of North America's coast found it a lush, virgin forest laced with cool-running rivers teeming with hearty stocks of salmon. These settlers treated their new home no better than they had their old, however. In less than two centuries, much of North America's forest had been cleared for lumber, fuel, and agriculture. The immediate result, an increase in water temperature, was only the first in a long line of environmental assaults that eventually brought the Atlantic salmon—once so plentiful it was used as fertilizer—to the verge of extinction in American waters.

INDUSTRY

New England's industrial revolution during the early nineteenth century was based primarily on water power, requiring dams, which blocked the salmon's passage to their spawning beds. Factories also introduced pollution and silt into the once-pure salmon waters. A factory on a salmon river inevitably resulted in total annihilation of that river's stock. Such thriving rivers as Maine's Kennebec, and New Hampshire and Massachusetts' Merrimack, lost all their Atlantic salmon. In 1798 a 16-foot (4.8-meter) dam was built across the Connecticut River at Hadley Falls, Massachusetts. At this time, nearly 4,000 fish could be taken with one haul of the nets at Old Saybrook Cove, near the river's mouth. When, in the early 1870s, a stray salmon was picked up in the shad nets at Old Saybrook, none of the fishermen could identify it. Dams built on the Merrimack River at Lawrence and Lowell, Massachusetts, in 1822 and 1847, respectively, were primarily responsible for ending runs numbering up to 30,000 fish annually. In a relatively few years, the afflictions of industry, compounded with commercial overfishing, had effectively exterminated the Atlantic salmon from most of New England.

Maine's salmon population suffered greatly as well, particularly from logging. River banks near hauling roads eroded, silting the salmon's spawning beds. Rivers often became congested with sawdust and wood debris, reducing oxygen levels. Paper mills released pulp and other pollutants into the rivers. The Penobscot River fishery, which had a reported catch of 15,000 fish in 1872, plummeted to a mere 47 fish in 1947. That same year, Maine's legislature established the Atlantic Sea Run Salmon Commission, which has pioneered salmon research and restoration. The Penobscot River restoration program has been tremendously successful, and has served as a model for all the New England restoration programs that followed. In 1986 nearly 5,000 fish were counted at the defunct Veazie Dam, and in 1990 anglers landed 1,000 Penobscot Atlantics, over half of which were then released.

Inspired by the success of the Penobscot restoration, the U.S. Fish and Wildlife Service—working with the Fish and Game Departments of Connecticut, Massachusetts, Vermont, and New Hampshire—began a salmon-restoration program on the Connecticut River in 1967. The river's dams were equipped with fish ladders, pollution was regulated, and hatcheries were built. The program obtained its fry and smolts from Maine's Penobscot, as this river most closely resembles the Connecticut's physical characteristics.

So far, returns on the Connecticut have been low (Table 9-1). This may be due in large part to the commercial fisheries off Greenland and Newfoundland (which have now ceased operation due to government and private buyouts). Precise figures are unknown, but one tagging study suggested as many as 50 percent of Connecticut River salmon were being lost to these fisheries. Pollution, which in recent years has decreased Long Island Sound's oxygen levels, is also a likely contributor.

A previous attempt at restoration, begun in 1867, was more successful (Buck, 1993). Planting fry from Penobscot River stock over a period of eight years resulted in the return of a few salmon. In succeeding years the numbers grew, but as soon as they did, gill nets appeared along the river and stake nets in the estuary. There was no regulation, licensing, or catch limits. A law passed to prevent taking these salmon until the upper tributaries were naturally restocked was widely disregarded, and it wasn't long before the river was once again barren.

The few returning salmon are selected by nature as those most fit to survive in the Connecticut River, and are critical to the restoration program's future. The fish are trapped, stripped of eggs and milt, and their progeny (as many as

TABLE 9-1

Returns of Adult Salmon to the Connecticut River During Restoration

1974 1	1978 90	1987 345	1992 489
1975 3	1979 175	1988 95	1993 175
1976 2	1981 529	1989 108	
1977 7	1986 318	1991 270	

500,000) are reared in the hatcheries and released into the river as smolts. Spawned-out females are kept to spawn again—some as many as five times. The ultimate goal of this painstaking process is to produce a well-adapted, self-sustaining stock.[1] The numbers involved show the dimensions of the problem: 8,000 eggs yield 4,500 alevin, which yield 650 fry, which yield 200 parr, which yield 50 smolts, of which only two survive to return as spawning adults.

Nor have Canadian salmon remained untouched by modern times. In 1957, during the spring runoff, a shut-down unit of the Heath Steele Mine was invaded by floodwater. The water was pumped into a feeder brook of the Tomoganops River, a tributary of the Northwest Miramichi. Unfortunately, the water was contaminated with highly toxic zinc and lead sulfides. For the membership of the Miramichi Fish and Game Club, catches on the Northwest rapidly declined until, with a 1968 tally of one salmon and four grilse, there was serious question whether the club should continue (Weeks, 1984). The poisons had not only wiped out returning spawners; it had killed the parr, and the insects on which they feed, as well. The latter two had hardly recovered from a spraying of DDT in 1953 aimed at killing the spruce budworm. It wasn't until 1972 that fish started returning in pre–1957 numbers, showing that the basic elements of recovery had finally reestablished themselves some four or five years before.

Commercial Fishing

A far greater threat to the salmon of North America and Europe arose from the discovery, in the late 1950s, that a major feeding ground for salmon lay off the west coast of Greenland, and later, that another one lay off the Faroe Islands between Norway and Iceland. Commercial shore and river fishing for salmon had been underway since the eighteenth century with little effect on the stocks, but now it became possible to net salmon in much larger numbers in their ocean feeding grounds, where fish from many countries were concentrated in a relatively small area. Tagging studies showed that fish migrating to Greenland came from Great Britain, Canada, and the United States. The Faroe Islands fish came primarily from Norway and Iceland. This situation presented a golden opportunity to Greenland's commercial fishing industry. Salmon would bring many times the price of cod—hitherto the staple of their trade. At about the same time, nylon nets became available. Because they were invisible to the fish, they were much more efficient than the twine nets they replaced. The drift nets, which could be as long as 17 miles (27 kilometers), were used in the open sea, while gill nets, which ensnared fish by tangling in their gill plates, were used inshore. Long lines of baited hooks were also used in the open ocean. In 1960, Greenland's fishermen landed 60 tons of salmon—barely enough to be a food supplement to its population of 50,000. By 1966 the catch had rocketed to 1,370 tons, and the Atlantic Salmon Federation called for the prohibition of high-seas fishing outside the Baltic area and the restriction of fishing to shore nets in territorial waters. But the next year, Greenland's fleet was joined by eleven high-seas trawlers: four from Denmark, three from the Faroe Islands (another Danish possession), and four from Norway. These boats added 314 tons to the take of 1,287 tons from the shore fishing, making the year's total 1,601 tons (about 441,000 fish). At its peak, the total ocean fishery (including the Newfoundland and Labrador shore fisheries) exceeded a half-million fish.

This was a dire threat to the future of the Atlantic salmon. At the 1968 meeting of ICNAF (the International Commission for the Northwest Atlantic Fisheries), Canada proposed the Greenland fishery be limited and regulated. This recommendation was supported by the United States and Great Britain. Denmark would not agree to the proposals. In the 1969 season, Denmark, now joined by Norwegian trawlers, brought the offshore drift-net catch to 1,358 tons. At the 1969 meeting of ICNAF, the United States proposed a complete ban on high-seas fishing for salmon, which was adopted despite opposition from Denmark and West Germany. Denmark ignored this mandate when fishing began that year, and actually increased its trawler fleet and took even more salmon.

Richard Buck, a passionate salmon angler, retired from a career in public relations while still in his fifties and soon thereafter began applying his skills and energy to salmon conservation. Buck was deeply involved in the campaigns to save the salmon from extinction by high-seas fishing, which he describes in his 1993 book *Silver Swimmer*. Salmon anglers everywhere are indebted to him for his leadership in this battle.

One of Buck's first accomplishments involved the organization of Project CASE (Committee on the Atlantic Salmon Emergency), whose purpose was twofold: to inform the general public of the serious threat to the salmon's future posed by the escalating Greenland fishery and inform what was being done to restore salmon in the United States. Because of the international scope of the issue, public support would be crucial in determining government diplomacy. Other key architects of CASE included the IASF (International Atlantic Salmon Foundation) and Trout Unlimited (TU). With help from a public-relations firm, CASE was very successful in obtaining media coverage—even more so when it enlisted the help of such salmon advocates as Bing Crosby, Ted Williams, Curt Gowdy, and Lee Wulff. CASE's treasurer, Dave Scoll, somehow persuaded the skipper of a Danish trawler to take a film crew to sea. The film shows the setting of a 17-mile-long (27 kilometers) drift net and its recovery the next day with a haul of salmon, along with great numbers of dead seabirds. The film caught the attention of the National Audubon Society.

The 1970 meeting of ICNAF sought to slow the escalation of the high-seas fishing by a proposal that would limit the 1970 high-seas catch to the level of 1969 and prohibit fishing for salmon outside national fishery limits by 1971. Denmark voted in favor, but still firmly opposed a total ban on high-seas fishing. The USSR, Iceland, Poland, and Canada voted against the proposal because they felt a total ban was the only solution to the problem.

Public opinion in Denmark was slowly shifting away from the rigid position taken by the government. After a "Save Our Salmon" dinner in January 1971 at New York's Waldorf-Astoria, representatives of Danish television interviewed some of the participants, including Bing Crosby, who was part Danish and very popular in Denmark. After the interview aired on Danish television, the Danish government retaliated by banning the sale of Crosby's records and the showing of his movies. However, the interview succeeded in changing a lot of minds in that country. Also contributing to the shift in Danish opinion was a CASE-organized trip to Copenhagen to discuss the situation with a group that included Denmark's Minister of Fisheries. The U.S. articulated its position and discussed a possible boycott of Danish goods. This was underscored later that year when Congress passed the Pelly Amendment, which authorized such a boycott. Here, strong support by the TU membership, the untiring lobbying of Richard Buck, and the support by the salmon-fishing members of Congress—Silvio Conte of Massachusetts and James Cleaveland from New Hampshire—were invaluable in putting pressure on the Danes.

In January 1972, Denmark's prime minister called for discussions among the interested parties (Canada declined to participate). The Danes agreed to phase out their high-seas salmon fishery over the four years from 1972 to 1975. The maximum *high-seas* tonnage would be 800 metric tons in 1972, 600 tons in 1973, 550 tons in 1974, and 500 tons in 1975. In 1976 they would terminate the high-seas fishing entirely. The *inshore* fishing by Greenlanders would be held to a maximum of 1,100 metric tons throughout. A major battle had been won, but the war was not over.

This agreement inspired further positive developments. Norway supported extension of its provisions to the whole ICNAF area and announced a total ban on high-seas fishing off its coast, to be put into effect by 1976. Soon after, Canada banned all commercial salmon fishing, including drift netting, in New Brunswick's territorial waters. It also called for a ban on all high-seas fishing for salmon, an action that was unpopular in Denmark. CASE, having accomplished its mission, was disbanded in 1973.

That same year, Richard Buck and many of the same people who had been active in CASE formed a second organization, RASA (Restoration of Atlantic Salmon in America). Among its many other activities, RASA supported legislative action to obtain funding for a hatchery and new fishways on the Connecticut River and for the design of fishways for dams on the Merrimack River at Lawrence and Lowell, Massachusetts.

After agreeing to a quota of 1,100 tons for Greenland's inshore fishing (in accordance with the 1972 ICNAF agreement), Denmark promptly violated this by taking 1,320 tons in 1972 and 1,547 tons in 1973. In addition, they tried to get the limit raised to 1,400 tons during the annual meeting of ICNAF in 1974, when they were already taking about 40 percent of the salmon migrating into Greenland waters. Due largely to Richard Buck's spadework, Denmark's proposal for 1,400 tons was rejected. Only Denmark and Japan were in favor.

With the extension of territorial limits on fishing to 200 miles (321 kilometers) by most nations, following the lead of the United States in 1976, there was no further role for the ICNAF, and it was disbanded. But this left migrating salmon unprotected in international waters. In June 1972, RASA called for an international organization to oversee and regulate the salmon resource globally. After years of negotiations between the salmon-producing and -consuming countries, in which Richard Buck again played a leading role (Buck, 1993), a treaty was finally signed in 1982. The signatories were Canada, Denmark (with respect to the Faroe Islands), the European Economic Community, Iceland,

Norway, Sweden, and the United States. This brought into being the North Atlantic Salmon Conservation Organization (NASCO), whose members would determine salmon-fishing regulations, particularly as they involved salmon originating in other jurisdictions. Richard Buck was named by President Reagan as one of the three United States commissioners to NASCO.

By 1983, the continued level of high-seas netting had so reduced the salmon stocks that Greenlanders were able to find only 250 tons of their quota of 1,191 tons, and the runs in the rivers were down by 50 percent or more. Under a 1993 NASCO agreement, the size of the Greenland quota was adjusted to ensure that all rivers would be able to fulfill their spawning potential.

During the late 1980s, two concepts became increasingly important to salmon conservation: (1) The exploitation of a river's salmon should occur in the river itself, or in its estuary, so that local people could be responsible for seeing that sufficient numbers of fish escaped to completely utilize the river's spawning potential. This is impossible when netting is carried out in the open sea, where fish from various rivers are mingled. (2) A salmon brings more money as a sport fish than it does as food. In 1984, no-kill angling regulations were enacted on all Canadian salmon rivers. Although catch-and-release did not have the dramatic effect on the salmon runs predicted by some, it undoubtedly reduced the declines of the stocks, and it was an important step symbolically.

In 1990, Orri Vigfusson, a native of Iceland and a dedicated salmon conservationist, organized the NASF (North Atlantic Salmon Fund), which bought out the rights to fish the NASCO quota for the Faroe Islands in 1991. In 1993, the NASF focused on Greenland. For $400,000, it bought out the rights to take 200 tons of salmon (all but 13 tons of the NASCO quota). Meanwhile, the Canadian government had declared a voluntary moratorium on the Newfoundland fishery, which included an offer to buy out the boats of native fishermen. The offer was widely accepted. In 1994, Vigfusson negotiated a three-year extension of the Faroe Island buyout.

Suspicions that high-seas drift netting for salmon was continuing were confirmed when vessels of Panamanian registry were found to be skippered by Danes, who were taking salmon in international waters of the North Atlantic. International pressure on Panama finally resulted in the "deflagging" of these ships.

All these positive measures have not resulted in the expected increase in the returns to the rivers, however. The reason for this is not known at this writing. One theory speculates that higher global temperatures have caused greater melting of the Arctic ice cap. The resulting increase in cold water may then have decreased the areas of the ocean having water temperatures of 39 to 46 degrees F (4 to 8 degrees C), which smolts require, and which attracts them to the Labrador Sea. Others note that, historically, salmon populations show cyclical variations, with minimums about every 40 years (1920 and 1960, for example). They anticipate that the year 2000 will be another low point, with recovery thereafter.

POACHING

If all these ravages aren't enough for the salmon to have to endure, poaching continues to this day. Most poachers either spear salmon at night or jig them with a weighted treble hook. In more remote areas, a team of poachers might net an entire pool. Since many poachers go uncaught, there's no telling how many fish they actually take. But considering that they often take fish right off the redds, the harm they do to the survival of the stock has to be considerable.

The principal deterrent to poachers is the presence of anglers. The proposal to make the Atlantic salmon an endangered species, which would eliminate sportfishing altogether, would result in a great increase in poaching.

THE SALMON'S FUTURE

Despite the successful restoration of some rivers and the rebound of salmon stocks, the Atlantic salmon's future is far from secure. At this writing, water diversions proposed by Quebec Hydro threaten the Moisie River, whose unusual stock of large fish make it one of the best salmon rivers in the world. Recently, Maine's Public Utilities Commission granted Bangor Hydro a permit to construct a dam on the Penobscot just north of Bangor, but the approval process is still subject to appeal, and the matter is presently unsettled.

Quota violations in the Canadian Indian subsistence fisheries continues to be a problem. If successful, the government-subsidized project on New Brunswick's Saint John River, which has put the Clearwater tribe into the outfitting business, may be extended to other tribes.

Clear-cutting in salmon rivers' watersheds continues, resulting in higher water temperatures and undesirable shifts in water level. A forested watershed absorbs heavy downpours, and slowly releases it to the groundwater, which in turn gradually feeds into the river and its tributaries. Clear-cutting results in erosion, causing much of the rainfall to run off unchecked into the rivers. Little water is stored as groundwater to compensate for drought periods.

Acid rain has already harmed some salmon rivers in Nova Scotia, and more will follow if the problem continues. If predictions of global warming prove correct, the future of the salmon is dark indeed. It is unthinkable that any coldwater fish could survive a greenhouse effect.

Such myriad threats to the Atlantic salmon suggest to some that the fish is certainly doomed. However, barring full-scale global warming, I think this pessimism is unwarranted. The salmon is now championed by large numbers of anglers, and they are well organized. In the last 25 years the salmon has benefited from the rise in conservation awareness initiated by the angler. The level of international cooperation in salmon preservation, so essential for a fish that ranges across national boundaries, is also on the rise.

The advent of aquaculture has made commercial netting only marginally profitable. Pen-raised salmon have drastically lowered the market price. Without this development, the buyout of the salmon fisheries off Newfoundland, Greenland, and the Faroe Islands would have been politically impossible. In addition, many former commercial fishermen now make their livings farming salmon. Many years ago Lee Wulff urged we declare the Atlantic salmon a gamefish and abolish commercial fishing for salmon entirely. The success of salmon aquaculture makes this suggestion much more feasible now than when he made it.

The Atlantic Salmon Federation (ASF) is an international nonprofit organization that promotes the conservation and wise management of the Atlantic salmon and its environment. ASF's national affiliates are the Canadian Wildlife Federation, the Federation of Fly Fishers, the Theodore Gordon Flyfishers, and Trout Unlimited. Through its regional council network in the United States and Canada, ASF represents thousands of anglers and conservationists. Councils include New England, Maine, New Brunswick, Prince Edward Island, Newfoundland, Nova Scotia, and Quebec. At this writing, the network comprises 117 organizations. The ASF concentrates its research, management, and educational programs in North America, but its commitment to the Atlantic salmon is international.

A regular membership in ASF ($40 U.S.) entitles you to a subscription to the *Atlantic Salmon Journal* (published quarterly). You will also receive *Salar*, a bilingual, tabloid-size newsletter reporting on ASF projects and giving catch numbers on various rivers both in North America and abroad.

I'M HOOKED! SIGN ME UP, NOW.

Name: _____

Address _____

City: _____

State/Prov.: _____ Country: _____

Zip/Postal Code: _____

Phone: _____

Select your Membership:
- ❏ Regular $40
- ❏ Affiliate $25
- ❏ Guide $25
- ❏ Student $25
- ❏ Library $25

- ❏ Sustaining $100
- ❏ Associate $500
- ❏ Sponsor $1,000
- ❏ Patron $5,000
- ❏ Benefactor $10,000+

Method of Payment ❏ Cheque ❏ MC ❏ Visa

Amount: $ _____

Credit Card #: _____

Expiry Date: _____

Signature: _____

Note: To qualify under the Affiliate or Student category, please indicate your school or affiliate organization. Guides please indicate license number: _____
Mail to: Atlantic Salmon Federation, Box 429, St. Andrews, NB, E0G 2X0 (in Canada), Box 807, Calais, Maine 04619 (in United States)
Canadian Registered Charitable Number: 0302059-54
U.S. Identification Number: 13-261-8801

Contributions are tax deductible in Canada and the United States according to law.   Rates expire December 31, 1995

Nearly every salmon river in North America has a club dedicated to its conservation and public-education projects (whatever river you fish, you will likely be invited to join its organization). Some of these activities are supported by grants from the ASF. Another source of funds are annual dinners held in the off season. Because of the large membership of the Miramichi Salmon Association (Central N.B. Woodmen's Museum Building, Boisetown, New Brunswick, Canada EOH 1AO), many of whom live in Massachusetts, its annual dinner, held in early February, attracts a large attendance. The ASF also hold an annual dinner, usually in April, in either Montreal or New York.

Below are listed some conservation organizations whose interests are more diverse, but who contribute to salmon conservation.

Trout Unlimited, 5001 Church Street NE, Vienna, VA 22180.

The Nature Conservancy, 1815 North Lynn Street, Arlington, VA 22209.

The Federation of Fly Fishers, P.O. Box 1088, West Yellowstone, MT 59758.

The American Museum of Fly Fishing, P.O. Box 42, Manchester, VT 05254.

NOTE

1. The newspapers carried a story in 1993 of a woman who reported seeing two large fish "fighting" in the Salmon River, a Connecticut tributary of the Connecticut River. Personnel from the Department of Environmental Protection who investigated, discovered the fighting fish were actually two spawning salmon—the first such occurrence recorded in the Connecticut River watershed in nearly a century and a half.

CHAPTER 10

Choosing an Outfitter

WHEN THE ATLANTIC SALMON NEARED EXTINCTION, MANY OUTFITters went out of business. When the runs improved, some of the camps[1] were purchased by private syndicates. Now that the runs have further improved, there are more camps catering to visiting anglers.

The best way to choose an outfitter is by taking the recommendation of someone whose opinion you trust. As with all things, the quality of salmon camps changes with time, so you need an up-to-date referral. In the better camps, satisfied clients return year after year, and make their reservations for the following year before they leave each season. Most camps have a confirmation deadline, by which time you must provide a substantial, nonrefundable deposit. If for some reason you cannot make your trip, you surely have a friend who'll be glad to take your place.

QUESTIONS TO ASK

A number of outfitters advertise in the *Atlantic Salmon Journal*. Maine, Quebec, and the Canadian Maritime Provinces all publish information as well (see Chapter 11 for addresses and telephone numbers). When you find a camp that interests you, there are a number of questions you should ask:

- How many pools does the camp control?
- What is the maximum number of rods that will be fishing these pools at one time? (The fewer anglers per pool, the more undisturbed water per angler.)
- What are the CPRD (catch per rod day; see below) numbers for the camp in recent years?
- Are there pools that fish well in high water?
- Is the fishing done all by wading, all from canoes, or both?
- Are licenses available in camp? If not, where can they be purchased?
- What are the mealtimes? The best arrangement is to have breakfast around 8:00 A.M., the main meal of the day around 1:00 P.M., and a light meal (sandwiches, etc.) after the evening fishing (9:30 to 10:00 P.M.). This allows you to fish the best hours—morning and evening—without missing meals, and leaves the least-productive early afternoon to eat the main meal of the day and to relax.
- Does the camp provide a map and explicit directions to the camp?
- Do you need a four-wheel-drive to get into camp?

- Are flies sold at camp? If not, how long a trip is it from camp to where you can buy them?
- Are there hot showers? If so, are they in the room or down the hall?
- Are there facilities in camp to ice fish for storage and transport? Can fish be smoked at camp?

The CPRD

CPRD (catch per rod day) is the only statistic we have to compare fishing success at different camps. A camp arrives at its CPRD by dividing the total catch of all anglers by the total number of angler-days involved. Suppose the number comes out to be 0.3. This means anglers caught 0.3 fish per day, or in other words, it took anglers an average of 3.3 days to catch one fish. How meaningful is such a number? As it is usually based on a voluntary questionnaire, not very. Perhaps the number of anglers queried was too small to be useful. The various provincial fish-and-game departments request anglers to record their catch data with them. This usually takes the form of an enclosure with the salmon license, and is supposed to be filled out and mailed in. And let's not forget that anglers are notorious liars. Some of them may have understated their catch to tell the Fish and Game Department there were far too few fish available. Others may have been telling fish stories. A day may be two hours for one angler and 12 hours for another. Surely the most accurate results are obtained when all caught fish are recorded by the camp owner.

Average CPRD numbers for Quebec's rivers varied considerably between 1984 and 1992. The lowest CPRD, 0.26, was chalked up on those rivers flowing into the Baie de Chaleur and those situated on the Gaspé Peninsula. The George, located at Ungava Bay in the far northern part of the province, was twice as good at 0.52. The best average, 0.63, was found on the lower North Shore rivers. The lowest single number belongs to the Laval at 0.10, and the highest to the Natashquan at 1.24.

But numbers only tell part of the story. Cost and ambiance aside, would you rather fish the Bonaventure, where the fish average 10 pounds (4.5 kilograms), or the Grand Cascapedia, where you seldom take a fish under 20 pounds (9.1 kilograms) (between 1984 and 1992, the CPRD averages of these two rivers were virtually identical: 0.31 and 0.32, respectively). Certainly you would rather fish the Grand Cascapedia. But when you factor in the price difference, even if you consider the ambiance equal, your decision might be changed.

At any rate, the CPRD is the best way we have to evaluate the potential of a camp that interests us. Here are some recent CPRDs of some of Quebec's other rivers: Patapedia, 0.13; Matane, 0.15; Jupiter, 0.70. Quebec publishes an exhaustive compilation of such data, while CPRDs for New Brunswick and Nova Scotia are generally unavailable. Maine and Scotland publish no such data. Where available, CPRDs for individual rivers and sections are included in Chapter 11.

SPATE RIVERS

If you are planning a salmon trip without using an outfitter, and are choosing a location based on CPRD numbers, be forewarned. There are many small salmon rivers, often referred to as *spate rivers*, that are fishable only a short time directly following a substantial rain. Salmon accumulate in the estuaries, waiting for a good rainfall to make their upstream passage possible. Although such a spate can occur during summer, they are more likely to occur in fall. When this happens, a multitude of fish suddenly appear in a stream that only days before had been barren. (The CPRDs of spate rivers, then, reflect only these days of extraordinarily good fishing, since nobody fishes them except after a rain.) Spate rivers are most productive for anglers who live nearby (see Bob Baker's description of the Jacquet River in Chapter 11).

Because of its limited drainage area, the streams of Anticosti Island, Quebec, are nearly all spate rivers. Table 11-6 shows that with adequate water levels they can provide excellent fishing. During a dry summer there may be no angling possible, however, at least on the smaller streams. Presumably the fish arrive on the spawning beds after the season has closed. If you are a visitor to the area and have limited time to spend, you must plan your trip around a major stream with a dependable flow. If there are spate rivers nearby, and a good rise of water occurs during your visit, they may provide a productive diversion. But they cannot be the sole focus of your trip (Ephraim Massey's discussion of Anticosti Island in Chapter 11 points up the dangers of reserving time on a spate river).

GUIDES

In New Brunswick and Newfoundland all nonresident anglers are required by law to have a guide. Elsewhere in Canada I'd advise you hire one if fishing a strange river—at least for the first few days until you learn its pools. Nearly all outfitters provide guides as part of the package. If not, you can arrange guide services through the outfitter by requesting one in advance.

A good guide can greatly increase your chances for success. An experienced guide has a detailed knowledge of your river: the best pools to fish and the best flies to use under given conditions, the best way to fish the pools, the location of lies, and the spots where wading is hazardous. Guides often compete to have their customer or *sport* be the most successful angler in camp. Out will come the favorite flies, often worn from the teeth of innumerable salmon, and often carried in an old tobacco tin. Theirs is knowledge based on many years of experience, a knowledge far too specific to be included in anything you may have read. If you have doubts about a fly your guide recommends, give it a good trial anyway. If it doesn't work, then make your own choice. While you are fishing, your guide may wander off to another pool to talk with other guides working there. This is not simply out of boredom. Your guide may bring back some information that will help you, or perhaps news of a fly that has been successful elsewhere on the river that day. Most guides have a repertoire of entertaining stories, which can relieve the tedium of fishless hours.

The beginning salmon angler should welcome the guide's taking the rod to demonstrate a cast or technique. This can get out of hand if the guides bring their own rods and fish alongside their sports. In fact, for a Class-1 guide to do so in New Brunswick is illegal. The arrangement whereby the guide hooks a fish and then turns the rod over to his sport makes little sense to me. The essence of salmon fishing lies in the challenge of getting the fish to take.

As a licensee of the state or province, the guide is charged with enforcing the game laws. Most guides take this responsibility seriously. By asking guides to look the other way as you violate a law, you are asking them to risk the loss of their livelihoods through loss of their license.

When to Go

The season for kelt or black salmon in New Brunswick runs from April fifteenth to May fifteenth. Bright salmon appear in the rivers during either the summer run, the fall run, or both. Although there is great variation among individual rivers, there is always salmon fishing somewhere in North America between June first and October thirtieth.

The earliest part of the summer run contains a higher percentage of large salmon (three- or four-sea-year fish and repeat spawners). Countering this is the fact that there are fewer of them. If you arrive too early, or if the salmon are delayed by ocean ice, you will have to wait for them, or you will have to be content with a very limited number of fish. By July first the summer run on most Canadian rivers (except those in the far north emptying into Ungava Bay) will be underway. The summer run will continue through July and extend into August. During August, the number of fish in the rivers falls off (except in the far north, when it may peak). The proportion of grilse in the summer run is low at the start, but increases as it proceeds. The fall run consists of stale salmon (fish that have taken the entire summer to move upstream) and, in increasing numbers, the fall run of bright fish. As water temperatures fall, the fish become darker as they develop eggs or milt.

The advantages of fishing the summer run certainly include the warm weather (sometimes too warm), fish that are more active and generally more likely to take, and greater opportunities for dry-fly fishing. The long evening hours, from when sun is off the water until dark, are generally productive. The disadvantages include pesky streamside insects (particularly the no-see-ums, on which most repellents are only moderately effective) and the possibility of poor fishing due to low and warm water.

In September when the evening hours are much shorter, the fish usually will take only a fly that is put right in front of them, and dry-fly fishing is less productive. However, pesky insects are scarce, and warm water is unlikely. In fact, when the frosts start, the lower water temperatures can make the fishing more difficult. High water is a possibility if you are hit by a September line storm or the remnant of a hurricane. Autumn fish have a reputation for fighting poorly. True, they are less inclined to jump, but they are strong, and will sometimes leap repeatedly (though not as much as summer fish). After a fall session I sometimes tell myself it will be good to get back to summer fishing. But then, after a summer session, I look forward to returning in the fall. The leaves change color during the last two weeks of September on the Miramichi, providing a colorful backdrop for your angling.

Reserving a week of salmon fishing is a considerable gamble. A number of things can conspire to make fishing difficult, if not impossible: high water; low, warm water; a poor run, or high losses of fish to poaching.

The least complicated way to make a reservation is directly through an outfitter. Dealing with specialized fishing-travel agents gives you an advantage in that they only book lodges meeting their high standards. They also facilitate the travel itself—a benefit when your destination requires several modes of transportation.

Specialized travel agents inspect fishing destinations worldwide, and will book you into the one you choose and arrange all travel. Having inspected your destination as recently as one year earlier, they can advise you on such matters as necessary clothing, equipment, and flies. These agents are paid by the lodge owners and transportation companies. One reputable fishing-travel agency is Frontiers, which made my trip to New Zealand trouble-free and enjoyable.

If you are driving directly to your destination you have little need of a travel agent. You have a much wider choice of camps and rivers, but you do not have the advice a good agent can provide. However, this is no problem if you get a recommendation from a reliable angler who has been there recently, or if the camp is one with which you're familiar.

The Quebec Reservation System

Making reservations in Quebec is considerably more difficult. Although sections of some rivers are still controlled by private outfitters, most accessible water is allocated to anglers by the MLCP (*Ministère du Loisir, de la Chasse et de la Pêche*). During the off-season, the MLCP holds a telephone lottery, selling fishing time on the various rivers, usually in three-day units. A lottery may be held by the MLCP (by telephone or mail), or by a ZEC (locally) for any particular river. A drawing is then held to determine which of the applicants will be allocated the fishing, lodging, or both. The daily rate varies according to the quality of the fishing and as to whether you are bidding for fishing rights only, or also for amenities such as lodging, meals, or even guides in canoes. In most cases, two or more sections of the same river may carry different price tags according to their quality. Rates are listed in the *Guide des Réservations de Pêche Saison* for the current year, which you can obtain from MLCP, Communications Office, 150, Boul. St. Cyrille Est, Quebec, Quebec G1R 4Y1, telephone 418-643-3127. For each river it lists (in French) the opening and closing dates, the dates of the lotteries, the telephone numbers for bidding, and the costs.

Note

1. Some outfitters make a distinction between fishing camps and fishing lodges. I don't consider this necessary, and therefore use the terms interchangeably.

CHAPTER II

The
Rivers

I N PLANNING YOUR SALMON-FISHING TRIP, THE FIRST ISSUE TO SETTLE IS THE budget, for there is a direct correlation between the CPRD (catch per rod day) of a river and the cost to fish it. Salmon fishing has a reputation as being only for the very wealthy. This is a holdover from days when the rivers were dominated by wealthy-sportsmen's clubs, a situation that is fading fast. It is still possible to spend a great deal for trips to a few locations on the North Shore of the St. Lawrence and to foreign destinations such as Iceland, Norway, and Russia (I recently priced a North Shore river having a CPRD of 0.73 at nearly $600 [U.S.] a day; the Canadian average is about $200). If you can afford bonefish at Christmas Island, or trout in Argentina or New Zealand, there are many excellent salmon locations with comparable prices and generally lower travel costs. For much less money you can fish on rivers with lower CPRDs and with amenities that are quite acceptable.

The following essays have attempted to provide current information on expenses, and to list sources for further information. As important as the fishing itself, I believe, are the intangibles of the location and its ambiance. To convey these I enlisted the help of a group of experienced salmon anglers, and asked them to write about the locations with which they are familiar. In reading them you will note they reiterate many points I've made in previous chapters.

Below is a map of the salmon-fishing areas of North America, minus Newfoundland. Detailed maps of each province will appear throughout the chapter.

THE MIRAMICHI RIVER SYSTEM

by Bill Cummings

The **Main Southwest Miramichi River** flows generally eastward from its origin about 20 miles (32 kilometers) from the Maine-New Brunswick border, and runs eastward about 150 miles (241 kilometers) across central New Brunswick to enter Miramichi Bay at Chatham. With its major tributaries—the **Cains**, the **Dungarvon**, the **Renous**, the **Little Southwest Miramichi**, the **North and South Sevogles**, and the **Northwest Miramichi**—each of which has its own stock of salmon, this is a vast watershed with the potential of producing a very large number of fish. The Miramichi has always attracted a large number of anglers from the United States because of its location just over the Maine border. In 1992 the angler catch of grilse (salmon must be returned and are there-

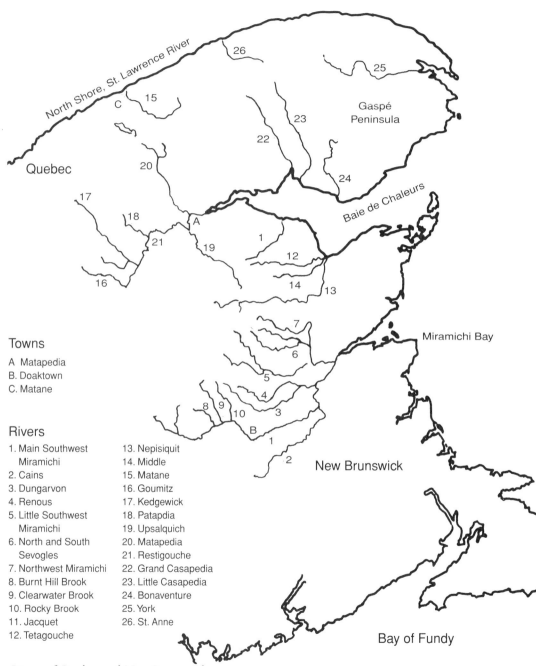

North Shore, St. Lawrence River

26

25

C 15

Gaspé
Peninsula

23

22

Quebec

20

24

17

A

Baie de Chaleurs

18

1

21

19

12

16

14 13

7

6

Miramichi Bay

Towns

A Matapedia
B. Doaktown
C. Matane

5

4

Rivers

8 9

10

3

1. Main Southwest
   Miramichi
2. Cains
3. Dungarvon
4. Renous
5. Little Southwest
   Miramichi
6. North and South
   Sevogles
7. Northwest Miramichi
8. Burnt Hill Brook
9. Clearwater Brook
10. Rocky Brook
11. Jacquet
12. Tetagouche

13. Nepisiquit
14. Middle
15. Matane
16. Goumitz
17. Kedgewick
18. Patapdia
19. Upsalquich
20. Matapedia
21. Restigouche
22. Grand Casapedia
23. Little Casapedia
24. Bonaventure
25. York
26. St. Anne

B

1

2

New Brunswick

Bay of Fundy

Rivers of Quebec and New Brunswick.

fore not counted) on the entire watershed was a reported 28,930 fish, of which 12 percent came from the tributaries. In addition, three other tributaries (they are called *brooks*, but would meet most peoples idea of a small river)—**Burnt Hill**, **Clearwater**, and **Rocky**—contributed to the diversity of the fish running the Main Southwest stem.

The flow in the lower part of the main river (below the Cains) is augmented by the water contributed from the six big tributaries. Because the river occupies a broad basin here, all the water contributed by these streams is spread out, resulting in a slow flow across a wide expanse of the main stream. There are many fishing camps here on both banks—mostly private, but a few are open to the public.

The middle section of the Miramichi, from the Cains River upstream to Boisetown, is still quite wide, but is characterized by the presence of islands and bars, which alter the flow to produce a variety of pools and other areas where the salmon can lie. With so many good places to fish, the river here is thickly settled with camps. There are a number of public camps just upstream from Blackville, especially from Doaktown through McNamee and Ludlow to Boisetown. If you are interested in the history of salmon fishing, Doaktown's Miramichi Salmon Museum is well worth an afternoon. Another Doaktown mecca is the Wallace Doak & Sons fly shop, where Jerry Doak continues the tradition begun by his father in catering to all the needs of New Brunswick's salmon anglers. Jerry's shop is one of the few that still carries low-water dressings.

Traveling upstream from Boisetown you'll hit a number of scattered fishing camps at Salmon Brook, Rocky Brook, Three Mile Rapids, and many more. As you proceed, the river becomes increasingly narrow, with more rapids and more large rocks, both on the shore and in the river itself. This is the most scenic section of the Miramichi, where you'll find yourself in a true wilderness setting. Many anglers prefer to begin far upstream at Half Moon Bay and gradually work their way toward civilization. Along the way you'll encounter lively rapids—Burnt Hill, Push-and-Be-Dammed, Company Line, Big and Little Louie, and the Narrows being among the more exciting ones. During low water, a scattered collection of fishing and camping gear may become fleetingly visible below these fast-water stretches, the wreckage of inexperienced river runners. You may be sure none of it belonged to clients of Miramichi guides.

The Miramichi was traditionally known as a grilse river. In the days of heavy commercial netting, the best fishing was had after the nets were lifted in

Miramichi fishing scene.

September. The commercial fishery was responsible for the high proportion of grilse. The nets, which were strung for miles along the lower river and estuary, had a mesh large enough to allow grilse to escape; thus, few big fish ever made it to the spawning beds. As Lee Wulff phrased it, this was analogous to a dog breeder disposing of champions and breeding only runts. With the nets now abolished (except for the Indian fishery), the ratio of grilse to salmon is about even.

The Black Brook Salmon Club is one of the organizations primarily responsible for starting a project that promises to make an important contribution to the full recovery of the Miramichi's salmon runs. At the suggestion of Arlie Wynn of the Miramichi Salmon Enhancement Center, the Black Brook Club embarked on a program of raising salmon fry (supplied by the Miramichi Fish Culture Station) to parr size in a cylindrical fiberglass tank. In the fall, when the fry have reached parr size, they are fin-clipped for identification and released into Black Brook. This program has been so successful that these so-called *satellite stations* have been installed at many such locations along the river.

Table 11-1 shows the significant improvement of the Miramichi watershed's fishing since 1980. This must be credited in large part to commercial fishing restrictions, the implementation of catch-and-release, and the buyout of the Newfoundland nets. As 1993 saw the virtual abolition of netting off Greenland's coast, salmon stocks both here and abroad should improve considerably.

TABLE 11-1

Grilse Catch in the Miramichi River System, 1981 to 1992

Year	Number	Rod-Days	CPRD
1981	4,985	24,259	0.21
1983	5,203	30,197	0.17
1984	10,536	32,406	0.33
1985	15,457	40,022	0.39
1986	29,746	59,974	0.50
1987	14,257	41,070	0.35
1988	17,795	42,199	0.42
1989	18,484	38,430	0.48
1990	15,413	35,146	0.44
1991	13,636	35,146	0.39
1992	28,930	43,754	0.66

While the tributaries provide only a relatively small portion of the salmon caught in the Miramichi basin, they make for the more intimate fishing experience preferred by some anglers. Table 11-2 compares their relative productivity during the 1981–1991 decade and 1992. In the calculation of the CPRDs in Table 11-2, the black salmon catch was included in the total. This was necessary since rod-days were not separated into bright fish and salmon categories. The Cains, Renous, and the Northwest Miramichi emerge as the tributaries with the more stable catches.

In his 1984 book *The Miramichi Fish and Game Club: A History*, Edward Weeks details fishing on the Northwest Miramichi throughout the years. He

TABLE 11-2

Relative Salmon Catch on the Miramichi Tributaries

River	Average[a]	1992
Cains	0.30	0.40
Dungarvon	0.26	0.22
Little Southwest	0.30	0.20
Renous	0.29	0.41
Sevogles	0.67	0.20
Northwest	0.59	0.69

a. Average CPRD for the years 1981–1991.

writes of the club's organization in the 1880s, the acquisition of leases on the Northwest, and the construction of fishing camps. He tells of the phenomenal fishing in 1906, when 17 or so club members landed 186 salmon and 53 grilse. Fish of 20-plus pounds (9.1-plus kilograms) were common then, and a few in the 30-pound (13.6-kilogram) range were taken. On a single trip, three brothers killed 27 salmon and 98 grilse.

Spraying DDT in 1952 to control the spruce budworm took a heavy toll on the Northwest's aquatic insects and salmon parr, resulting in a dramatic decline of adult fish in subsequent years. In 1957, pollution emitted from the Heath Steele Mine so devastated the area's salmon stock that by 1968 the club's season total was only one salmon and four grilse, giving serious thought to club members of closing operations.

The Miramichi is one of the few rivers on which there is extensive fishing for kelts. The season runs from April 15 to May 15. Opinion is divided whether this harms salmon conservation. The traditional method of fishing for kelts is to sit in an anchored boat and pay out a sinking line and some backing, and then slowly reel in. The flies are large, bright-colored streamers. A more sporting alternative has been championed by Gary Anderson, who says kelts can be caught by a wading angler using a floating line. He also objects to the notion they do not fight well, and that fishing for them endangers the stock (see the *Atlantic Salmon Journal*, Winter 1987). George Gruenefeld, on the other hand, after his first experience kelt fishing with Anderson, likens it to "teasing old men."

Traditionally, most fly patterns used on the Miramichi were black. The Black Bear series, dating back to 1935, and Ira Gruber's Gorilla have been standards, varying only in the number and color of their butts. If my experience is typical, an angler happens upon butt-color preference by chance. You get into a bunch of taking fish, land as many as four or five in an hour, and whichever color butt you were using at the time becomes your favorite. I ended up with a preference for reddish orange.

Miramichi anglers eventually learned that other colors produced well on their river. Years before he invented the Bomber, Father Elmer Smith had excellent results with a predominantly white fly he originated. Named "The Priest" (not by Father Smith), this fly soon became a standard at the Doaks' fly shop, among a number of others.

Another effective Miramichi pattern with a good share of white is the Butterfly. For a long time it was the best-selling fly in the Doaks' shop. I always carry a good supply.

The Undertaker is another good Miramichi pattern. With a bear-hairwing and a peacock-herl body, it's basically a dark fly, although its two tips—one green and the other orange—brighten it significantly. In my experience it will outfish a traditional black fly, such as the Black Squirrel-Orange Butt, which is no slouch itself. I believe the glint of the herl body and the fly's liveliness in the water play an important role in its effectiveness.

The Green Machine ousted the Butterfly as the Miramichi's top-selling fly. Some anglers fish the Machine exclusively throughout the season. This is a bit rigid for my taste, but it shows the degree of confidence this fly can inspire.

Salmon appear in the Miramichi in June, but in small numbers compared with the hordes of July. Extensive clear-cutting on the river's watershed has made it more susceptible to extremes of flow. This makes it a bigger risk to choose a week's stay, particularly on the main stem. During very hot and extended dry spells, Canadian officials may close the river, as salmon weaken under these conditions, and are unlikely to survive a fight with an angler. Another consideration is the danger of a major forest fire. Officials sometimes close woodland regions until a heavy rain soaks them well.

The summer run tapers off during August. Fishing picks up again during early September as the cooler waters start the fish moving. In recent years, the Miramichi's season has closed on October 7.

For more information about fishing New Brunswick, call 800-561-0123.

THE NEPISIGUIT AND OTHER AREA RIVERS

by Bob Baker

Long renowned for its Atlantic salmon, the Nepisiguit River flows some 80-plus miles (129-plus kilometers) east and north from the Bathurst Lakes through northern New Brunswick to enter the Bay of Chaleur at Bathurst. In the 1600s, the explorer Nicholas Denys complained in his journal of "the incessant splashing of the salmon" keeping his men awake at night while camped by the river.

The first recorded instance of fly-fishing on the Nepisiguit was in August of 1845, when two Bathurst residents and two British officers visited the pools below Grand Falls. Despite having only one canoe and one gaff, they managed to land a total of 90 salmon and 13 grilse in two days.

Only the lower 18 miles (29 kilometers) of the Nepisiguit are accessible to salmon, their passage blocked by the 80-foot (24-meter) Grand Falls. With the river's drop of some 600 feet (183 meters) in those 18 miles (29 kilometers), salmon pools abound, over 90 of which have names.

Historically, much of the river was under private lease, and angling catches averaged about 800 fish per season through the 1940s and 1950s, declining to 600 in the 1960s as commercial overfishing at sea began to take its toll. In 1969, heavy acidic rainfall, together with sulfide dumping by a local mining operation, combined to create a toxin that wiped out the juvenile population in the main stem while keeping mature fish from entering the river. Several years passed before this was cleaned up and the system was flushed, during which time few salmon were present. In 1974 a few salmon, descendants of those that survived in the Nepisiguit's tributaries, returned in the fall.

In 1976 a group of local anglers formed the Nepisiguit Salmon Association (NSA) with a goal to rebuild the salmon stocks. Assisted by the Federal Department of Fisheries and Oceans, the NSA initiated a formal salmon-enhancement program in 1981. They constructed a 700-foot-long (213-meter) counting/collection fence, with which they conducted juvenile-salmon surveys and collected brood stock. Funded through various grants and agencies and aided by contributions from industry, this program continues today. In 1985, in cooperation with Brunswick Mining and Smelting and the Noranda Technical Centre, the first streamside incubation box for Atlantic salmon was tested on Pabineau Brook, a subsidiary stream in the Nepisiguit system. Twenty-five thousand eggs achieved 96-percent hatch rate. Since then, the NSA's hatchery program has been moved to the Stone Hydro site, and expanded to an annual production of 350,000 eggs, which average over a 95-percent hatch rate. This is *five to 10 times* the natural rate.

Nepisiguit fishing scene.

As a result of the efforts of the NSA and the Department of Fisheries and Oceans, angling has steadily improved on the Nepisiguit, with the catches in most years now exceeding those enjoyed over 50 years ago. With the bulk of the commercial salmon fisheries bought out, there is an opportunity to finally achieve a self-supporting salmon run.

At present, the best fishing is usually during the first two weeks of July, and then during the month of September and continuing until the season closes on October seventh. Table 11-4 illustrates angling success rates in recent years.

With two exceptions—the water directly below Grand Falls, which is owned by Stone Consolidated and leased by a local angling club, and the waters held by the river's only outfitter, Joan and Ken Gray at the Nepisiguit River Camps—the river is open to public angling. While some favorite spots are a bit crowded, there are a sufficient number of large pools to provide quality angling.

If you prefer to operate without an outfitter, or are unable to book at your

TABLE II-3

Annual Catch and Release, Nepisiguit River, 1981 to 1992

Year	Catch			Release		Grand Total
	Grilse	Salmon	Total	Grilse	Salmon	
1981	285	40	325		75[a]	400
1982	629	95	724		104	828
1983	240	60	300		60	360
1984	600	0	600	150	150	900
1985	500	0	500	100	300	900
1986	800	0	800	400	500	1,700
1987	800	0	800	550	500	1,850
1988	1,000	0	1,000	400	700	2,100
1989	600	0	600	100	500	1,200
1990	500	0	500	100	300	900
1991	700	0	700	150	300	1,150
1992	800	0	330	270	1,400	

a. total of salmon and grilse.
Average catch (1982–1992): 1,208; Average release: 391 salmon/518 grilse

TABLE II-4

Angling Summary, Nepisiguit River, 1990 to 1992

Month	Year	Grilse	Salmon	Total	Rod-Days	CPRD
June	1990	15	30	45	400	0.11
	1991	15	20	35	300	0.12
	1992	15	25	40	300	0.13
July	1990	40	15	55	400	0.14
	1991	70	25	95	600	0.16
	1992	170	25	195	800	0.24
August	1990	65	35	100	400	0.25
	1991	105	25	130	500	0.26
	1992	300	50	350	1,000	0.35
September	1990	380	170	550	1,500	0.37
	1991	525	180	705	1,700	0.41
	1992	475	120	595	2,000	0.30
October	1990	95	50	145	700	0.21
	1991	135	50	185	600	0.31
	1992	160	50	210	600	0.35

preferred times, there are a few local guides who may be available—though I emphasize the word *few*. You can usually contact them through the local Department of Natural Resources, P.O. Box 170, Bathurst, New Brunswick, E2A 3Z2, telephone 506-547-2080. There are numerous motels in Bathurst that are only a short drive from the river.

While short compared with many salmon rivers, the Nepisiguit is quite a large river in total surface area, and your rod should be no shorter than 9 feet (2.7 meters). Some local anglers fish with 10-foot (3-meter) rods. You can expect wind in the fall, so I'd advise you use a nine-weight line then. Few parts of the river are excessively deep, and the water is quite clear. Therefore, sinking lines are seldom necessary—a weight-forward floating line is the standard. One hundred yards (94 meters) of backing is usually sufficient, though the occasional 25- to 30-pound (11.3- to 13.6-kilogram) fish makes 150 yards (137 meters) of backing a better idea.

Popular fly patterns of the Nepisiguit include the Black Bear series, Cosseblooms, Rusty Rats (for sunny days), a full range of Buck Bugs, Bombers (normally fished wet on the Nepisiguit), the universal Blue Charm, the Undertaker, the Nepisiguit Gray, and other locally developed patterns such as the Half and Half, the Nepisiguit Green, and the Eclipse. It goes without saying you should also bring flies in which you have confidence.

The Nepisiguit is generally a big-fly river, with popular sizes being 4 and 6 (seldom below 8). Streamers tied on size-2, 6XL hooks are quite successful, particularly in the fall. The Black Ghost is one of the favorites. Dry flies are quite productive in July and August, particularly the Wulff series and the Miramichi Bombers. If water temperatures are warmer than normal (50 to 59 degrees F [10 to 15 degrees C]), these flies can produce in September as well.

Other Area Rivers

There are several smaller rivers in the area that can provide salmon fishing, although most need good water conditions to produce (such rivers are called *spate* rivers). Thirty miles (48 kilometers) north of Bathurst is the **Jacquet River**, which can afford excellent fall angling if its water is high (its season runs to October 15). On October 12, 1991 I hooked five salmon and two grilse in six hours of fishing there using streamers. The **Tetagouche River**, near Bathurst, can have good runs in late September and early October, as can the **Nigadoo** and **Middle Rivers**. These rivers are quite small compared with the Nepisiguit. Local anglers have the advantage in that they can wait for the necessary rains—a luxury not afforded visitors.

THE MATANE

by Bill Cummings

Quebec's Matane River flows northwest from Lake Matane, then north across the Gaspé Peninsula, entering the Gulf of St. Lawrence at the town of Matane. U.S. residents can reach it by crossing the border at Van Buren, Maine, and following New Brunswick's Route 17 to Matapedia, Quebec. From there, follow the Matapedia River north on Route 132 to Amqui, from which Route 195 takes you into the Valley of the Matane along the east bank of the river to the town of Matane on the coast. The dam near the river's mouth includes a fish ladder. A glass-walled chamber through which you can view the ascending salmon is a popular tourist attraction. All entering salmon are counted here, and the tally is posted daily.

You do not need a daily permit to fish the lower part of the river—section 1, pools 1 through 5—but you do need a Quebec salmon license. Upriver of section 1 is section 2, a 3-mile (4.8-kilometer) sanctuary where you may fish only with permission of the landowner. The next 25 miles (40 kilometers) along Route 195—section 3, pools 12 through 79—is where most of the Matane's fishing is done. Up to pool 46, where Route 195 crosses the river, the pools are within reasonable walking distance of the highway. Pools 47 to 60 are on a paved road that follows the Matane upstream. This leads to a camping area and the entrance to a Provincial Park (Réserve Matane), through which you can access the remaining pools by a gravel road. To fish pools 12 to 79 you must have a daily permit ($41.56 Canadian for nonresidents) and a Quebec Salmon License ($62.68 Canadian for nonresidents). You may obtain licenses and permits at 257 Rue St. Jerome in the town of Matane. Permits are also available at the town of St. René de Matane about 12 miles upriver. All fish killed must be tagged and registered at one of these locations.

When the Paper Company deeded its property rights to the province, after cutting the riverbank timber, they stipulated that the public must have free access to the river across 200-foot (61-meter) strips on both banks (later reduced to 30 feet or 9 meters). This has not always been a popular arrangement with the owners of streambank property. Unfortunately, the inconsiderate behavior of some anglers (littering, trampling gardens, etc.)—some of whom are American—has only compounded this resentment.

With 79 available pools, you might suppose you'd have no problem finding productive water. In fact, most of the fishing is done on these major pools: Les

Cedres (15), Les Tufs (16), Le Cran Rouge (17), Johnson (18), La Côte à Tuer*
(20), LeBreux* (23), Le Panier* (25), Le Ruisseau Gagnon (26), La Vielle (27),
La Petite Matane* (or Metropole, as it is often called, referring to a nearby hotel)
(28), La Fosse Rouge (31), La Becateron (44), Le Petite Tamogadi (45), Le
Grand Tamogadi (53), La Fumeuse (55), Le Cap Seize (57), La Côte de
Glace* (63), Le Vieux Tentage (67), La Côte aux Pêches (72), La Cage (78), and
La Truite (79). Pools marked with an asterisk tend to be overcrowded, especially on weekends and holidays. There are many pools besides those listed that
can provide good fishing, but most of them produce well only at very specific
water levels. Since there is no limit to the number of daily permits issued, and
since rotation is rarely organized, the situation can become chaotic, especially
during a good run of fish.

Table 11-5 shows that the Matane had rather poor fishing in the eight years
preceding 1992, and only a moderate improvement in that year. Elsewhere,
1992 was generally a good year due to the Newfoundland net buyout as well as
favorable weather.

TABLE 11-5

Fishing Success on the Matane River, 1984 to 1992

Year	Catch	Rod-Days	CPRD
1984	670	4,489	0.15
1985	616	4,580	0.13
1986	864	6,716	0.13
1987	743	6,100	0.12
1988	978	6,174	0.16
1989	173	1,711	0.10
1990	837	5,289	0.16
1991	854	5,165	0.17
1992	1,325	6,710	0.20

Accommodations for the angler visiting the Matane include the Bell Plage
Motel in Matane; a camping area beside pool 25; The Metropole Hotel at pool
28; some overnight cabins at pool 46, where Route 195 crosses the river; and the
camping and RV facilities at the gate of Réserve Matane. The Bell Plage is the
most expensive of these, and decidedly the most comfortable. However, it's a
good distance from the most frequently fished pools. The camping at pool 25
puts you right on the banks of Le Panier, a good pool. The provincial camping

at Réserve Matane is well located, especially if you plan to fish the park pools frequently. I cannot comment on the other hotels and camping areas as I have never stayed in them.

Fed by Lake Matane, the Matane River has a fairly steady flow rate that seldom sees extremes. The upper part of its watershed—above pool 60—is heavily wooded, including the environs of a major tributary, **Trout River**, which enters at pool 79. This also contributes to steady flow and moderate river temperatures.

As salmon rivers go, the Matane is relatively small. If you are a reasonably good fly-caster you can cover its pools thoroughly by wading. The cost of a daily permit encourages you to fish every possible moment, including the least-productive afternoon hours. Competition for a spot on a major pool before it has been thoroughly worked over causes some anglers to purchase their permit the day before and to arrive on the scene before dawn—in some cases, well before dawn.

In all the years I've fished the Matane I've never found a fly that consistently outperforms the rest. In looking through my fishing diaries, I see these names most often: Cosseboom, Oriole, Black Bear-Green Butt, Mickey Finn, Silver Rat, Butterfly, Colburn, Rusty Rat, Orange Blossom, White Wulff, and MacIntosh.

Before starting to fish the Matane, pay a visit to George Maul's Fly Shop at 270, Route 195 in the little village of St. René de Matane. George has been fishing the river for many years. He has a great display of salmon flies as well as equipment of all sorts.

THE RESTIGOUCHE

by Bill Cummings

The Restigouche River forms the border between New Brunswick and Quebec as it flows northeast to the Baie des Chaleurs near Campbellton, New Brunswick. Before reaching the sea it is joined by the **Goumitz**, the **Kedgewick**, the **Patapedia**, the **Upsalquich**, and the **Matapedia**—all but the first of which are major salmon rivers in their own right. In June of 1992 I fished the Restigouche out of the Red Pine Mountain Lodge, which is reached by a gravel road from St.-Jean-Baptiste, New Brunswick. The road ends at the banks of the river at Two Brooks Landing, where the Warden's Camp is located. From there, one of the guides transports you and your luggage to the Lodge in one of

Restigouche fishing scene.

the 26-foot (7.9-meter) fishing canoes equipped with an outboard motor.

This was a new fishing experience for me—a veteran of the tough fishing on the overcrowded Matane in the 1960s and 1970s, and a persistent optimist facing the small runs on the Miramichi before the no-kill regulations of the 1980s. I was about to fish drops from a canoe—something I had not done since I had first started salmon fishing in 1958. My roommate and I shared a guide who knew exactly where to position us in this large river, which was running high at the time. There are several advantages to canoe fishing: It is not physically demanding; you can be sure you are covering the water in the best possible manner; and you have the help of an experienced guide who knows the effective local patterns, and knows how you should best play and land your fish.

The Restigouche is well known for its higher proportion of larger fish—especially in June. Joseph Pulitzer II fished it for 39 years—from 1915 to 1954—27 of them out of Mortimer Schiff's Brandy Brook Camp. Pulitzer's best year was reportedly 1930, when his party took 329 salmon between June 6 and July 13. On July 24, 1949 he landed a salmon of 41 pounds (18.5 kilograms). In August of 1987, fishing at **Brandy Brook** in extremely low water, Joseph F. Cullman III hooked a tremendous salmon on a size-8 Green Highlander. The fish took 70 minutes to land. Cullman measured the fish before releasing it, and according to the Ward Formula (see Appendix A) it weighed an estimated 46 ½ pounds (21 kilograms). The official lodge record is 47 pounds. With all this fresh in my mind, the possibility of taking a fish of over 30 pounds (13.6 kilograms) did not seem too remote. Such a trophy had eluded me for many years.

Fishing on the Restigouche is controlled by members of the Restigouche Salmon Club and the owners of a few other private lodges. They take good care of it by employing the wardens to prevent poaching and netting. The Restigouche had suffered from the commercial netting and the Indian subsistence fishery in the 1980s, but when these afflictions sapping the stock were controlled, fishing improved. Charlie Zell says that of the 240 fish landed by anglers at Red Pine Mountain Lodge in 1992, four were over 40 pounds (18 kilograms) and 12 were over 30 pounds (13.6 kilograms). And yes, one of those 30-pounders was mine!

The facilities at Red Pine are excellent, and the food is delectable. The fishing occurs in two sessions: 8:00 A.M. to noon, and 5:30 to 9:30 P.M. This is an ideal fishing arrangement, and also allows for a reasonable meal schedule, including a buffet before the evening fishing and a snack afterwards. The guides are first-rate and the camp management is unfailingly helpful.

For more information on Red Pine Mountain Lodge, contact Doug Schlink at Angler Adventures, P.O. Box 827, Old Lyme, CT 06371, Tel. 203-434-9624 or 800-628-1447; FAX 203-434-8605.

THE RIVERS OF THE NORTH SHORE AND ANTICOSTI ISLAND

by Ephraim Massey

The first good salmon river on the North Shore of the St. Lawrence beyond Quebec City is the **Ste. Marguerite**. It's a short drive from the pretty town of Tadoussac (famous for its whale watching). A true sense of remoteness comes

Scene of North Shore fishing, as on the Moisie.

over you as you cross the Saguenay River by boat. The Ste. Marguerite is just beyond the sleepy village of Sacré-Coeur. It's a small, friendly river, and the access is easy as the main road follows it closely with most pools well marked. Some are best fished by canoe, particularly early in the season and during high water. This river is very similar in character and appearance to the Ste. Anne in the Gaspé.

The Ste. Marguerite is run by a ZEC or *Zone d'exploitation Controlé*, a local government-supervised fishing club. Reservations on two sections are on a lottery system. As with other Quebec rivers, the lottery may be held live for a fishing period 48 hours later, or may be by telephone or mail during the winter. Each bid receives a number. A drawing is then held, limited by the available space, to decide who will fish. The other sections accept an unlimited number of rods. On my last trip there, in 1990, Richard Barbacki and I landed three 10-

to 12-pound (4.5- to 5.4-kilogram) salmon in four days. All were hooked at Glass Pool in section 4, and one was landed at Brisson, the pool below. We arrived there in late June, which is considered prime time, though the river was low. During our stay it rained hard and the river rose steadily. We started off with small flies and ended up fishing with big Magog Smelt Bucktails. As on many other rivers, black flies and green ones seemed to be the anglers' favorites. Large salmon are sometimes caught here, but not often.

Farther along the North Shore, heading northeast, is the **Laval** in Forestville, which I have never fished. It is run by the Forestville ZEC. Each time I pass, I make a mental note to try it the following year. Not many fish are caught in the Laval (CPRD is 0.10), but they average close to 20 pounds (9.1 kilograms). There is little demand for reservations because the access is difficult, and the best fishing is restricted to high-water periods in June.

The lower **Grand-Trinité** can be good when the salmon runs are on. However on the lower sections you must fish from small designated areas—usually planks or rocks. You may cast as much line as you wish, but you are not allowed to go into adjacent areas. Sometimes these areas are close together; other times, not. It doesn't sound very interesting, and it isn't—unless of course you are into a salmon. Sometimes, as when I fished there in late July a few years back, it can be quite pathetic. The upper river is reportedly quite different and very pleasant to fish, though I have not seen it.

I haven't fished the **Godbout**, but I hear from friends that the situation is similar to that on the Grand-Trinité. Nevertheless, these rivers are very popular, particularly among the locals.

The **Moisie**, just beyond Sept Iles, is one of the truly great salmon rivers. The lower section is controlled by a ZEC, and there is unrestricted access in portions. Anglers can troll hardware below the bridge, but must use fly gear above it. In 1988, I fished the Winthrop-Campbell section of the ZEC, which used to be private water belonging to the Moisie Salmon Club. This water was frequented by American and Canadian politicians, including President Eisenhower and several Quebec premiers. At $40 per rod (*this and other prices in this section are Canadian dollars*) it's a real bargain (limit three fish per day). Passes are awarded by lottery—some on mail-in lottery and the others by an on-site system. The fishing is not easy, however. You'll need a good motorboat or canoe, and unless you know the area, the pools are difficult to locate and fish. I highly recommend a guide for the first day or two.

Richard and I fished from his Zodiak (a type of inflatable rubber boat). For the first two days we watched other anglers to get a sense of where and how to fish. In four days of fishing I landed two salmon weighing 16 and 18 pounds (7.3 and 8.2 kilograms). Both fought hard and took lots of backing. I hooked them after casting all day in the same area. The Moisie is a wild, beautiful river. It's no wonder there's been so much opposition to Quebec-Hydro's plan to dam its main tributary.

Fishing the river above the ZEC is another matter. This is private club water, and it's expensive, though the fishing is generally superb at all the camps. At Blanchette Pool, anglers are flown in from Sept Iles by helicopter for the day. Guides and lunch are provided. There are also camps such as Moisie Nipissis Outfitters, where anglers can have full room and board while they fish.

Farther along the North Shore, and closer to Havre St. Pierre, is the **Rivière St. Jean**. (Two smaller rivers in Quebec share the name—one in the Gaspé and the other on the lower North Shore.) It's a big river like the Moisie, but is less well known and has smaller fish. Most of the river is controlled by a local club. There are different sectors with various packages available. In 1993 we fished there for three days in late June, normally considered prime time. A minivan picked us up at our motel in the town of Rivière St. Jean and drove us to the river, where we met our guides. In the morning the pools are divided among eight rods—two rods per pool. In the afternoon they rotate. Most pools are fished by canoe, though several can be waded. The scenery is so beautiful that hooking a salmon is a bonus.

In three days we caught nothing, though my friend had one strike. The water was very low and there were few fish in the river—quite unusual for late June.

Two years earlier was a different story. We hooked seven fish, landing four from 9 to 13 pounds (4.1 to 5.9 kilograms). One of our party landed a 23-pounder (10.4 kilograms) at Black Rock. Unfortunately, this pool, by far the best on that section, was removed last season from the rotation.

The St. Jean has lodges above and below the guided section where the fishing is offered on the American Plan (that is, the price includes meals). Prices here are comparable with those charged on the Moisie and the Grand Cascapedia, though the fishing is probably not as good.

Some of my best memories are of the **Natashquan**. I went there as a guest of the Hipu Outfitters in mid-July of 1986. It is owned and run by the Montagnais tribe of Indians. This tremendous river has an incredible run of salmon, probably over 100,000. I flew to Natashquan from Sept Iles and went upriver by motorboat. Natashquan is a picturesque fishing village full of character.

There are two comfortable lodges on the Natashquan. Fishing centers around the sets of large waterfalls where the salmon congregate. I stayed at the upper lodge and fished a few days around the Third and Fourth Falls, hooking mostly grilse. I had better fishing on my last day, around the lower camp, though I found the scenery nicer higher upriver. Here your chances for larger fish are better in June.

Much has been written about Anticosti Island, and I had the opportunity to fish there in 1987. In the late 1890s it belonged to one man, Henri Menier, the chocolate millionaire from France, who ran it as a sort of fiefdom. Later it was owned by a paper company. It now belongs to the Quebec government, and is maintained for hunting, fishing, and limited tourist activities.

TABLE 11-6

CPRD of the Rivers of Anticosti Island

River	1987–1991	1992	River	1987–1991	1992
Jupiter	0.70	0.42	Dauphiné	1.17	a
MacDonald	0.42	0.29	du Rernard	b	a
Patate	0.33	0.34	Maccan	b	a
Vauréal	0.19	0.32	Ferée	1.01	0.90
aux Saumons	0.51	0.43	Martin	1.11	0.69
de la Chaloupe	0.53	0.59	du Pavillon	b	a
Becscies	0.20	0.18	aux Plats	b	a
Ste. Marie	0.20	0.18	Chicotte	0.91	0.29
de la Loutre	b	a	Galiote	0.52	0.32
Bell	0.72	a	du Brick	0.13	a
Box	0.81	a			

a. Not fished in 1992.
b. Not fished in this period.

Anticosti is a beautiful, desolate place. There are cliffs, forests, and long beaches populated by seals. Deer are everywhere. You can still see several shipwrecks around the island. Sadly, most of the old buildings and lighthouses were torn down or have collapsed. The Menier "chateau" burned down in the 1950s.

I crossed the St. Lawrence on the ferry from Havre St. Pierre to Port Menier. I was traveling with my wife and two small children. Our first stop was the **Rivière à Patate**, where we had booked several days of fishing along with a government chalet. Unfortunately, the area was experiencing a drought. The river was a small brook. I saw two grilse at the tidal pool when we arrived. The next day they were gone. We spent most of our time sightseeing. We explored the shipwreck near the Patate and walked along the canyon of the **Vauréal River** to the falls. They are higher than the Niagara Falls and there is a beautiful deep pool at the foot of the falls where Charlie MacCormick, former caretaker of the island, described seeing numerous salmon jumping. We also visited some of the Patate caves. I fished for a day on the **MacDonald**, but the water was so low the salmon were jammed into small pools and were spooked whenever a fly landed nearby. A few were caught while we were there, but I suspect they might have been jigged.

I spent a day with a government guide on the **Jupiter,** and I can see why it is synonymous with salmon fishing on Anticosti. It is one of the very few substantial salmon rivers on the island, and anglers at the lower camp generally have excellent salmon fishing throughout the season. The fish are not large—they average about 10 pounds (4.5 kilograms)—but they are plentiful. Some pools may hold 100 salmon.

Anglers used to be pulled up the Jupiter in horse-drawn scows; today they use trucks. The river is surrounded by tall granite cliffs and the water is pale emerald. Both the Ten Mile and the Thirty Mile camps are luxurious, with gorgeous views. The accommodations and food are excellent. All angling packages on the Jupiter include guides. It's not cheap; a day's fishing runs into the hundreds, not including transportation. However, when water levels are low on other Anticosti rivers, the Jupiter has enough water to hold fish, and it's unusual for an angler to get skunked.

I spent a few days on the **Chalupe River**, and landed a lively grilse just before nightfall at Home Pool beside the camp using a size-10 Black Bear-Green Butt. We fished for two days at the mouth of the river and caught many sea-run trout, but never landed a salmon. Most of the time we used size-16 dry flies. Some of the pools contained scores of salmon, but they showed no interest in our flies. The river was extremely low and the water warm. During higher water the fishing here is reportedly excellent.

There are many other salmon rivers on Anticosti, but most are spate rivers. There is also excellent sea-run trout fishing in many of the streams, and also from some of the beaches near the river mouths.

Michel Fournier is in charge of SEPAC ANTICOSTI, which rents out fishing, accommodations, chalets, etc. For more information, contact Michel at 3000 Rue Alexandra, # 102, Beauport, Quebec G1E 7C8, Tel. 418-890-0863.

THE RIVERS OF THE GASPÉ PENINSULA

by Ephraim Massey

Most of my salmon fishing in Quebec has been on the Gaspé Peninsula. One of my favorites is the **Patapedia**, a small sister to the Matapedia. The Patapedia is wild and holds big salmon. Sadly, though, the runs have decreased in the last few years. Nevertheless, I return every year. The Patapedia flows into the Restigouche's famous Million Dollar Pool.

Last summer we fished three days in early July on the top section. Water levels were low. Not one fish had yet been taken, and the other four rods had canceled. In three days we saw two salmon at Blueberry Pool, but never rose a fish. We had better luck on the three-day canoe run; each of us took several salmon, and also a few grilse. This portion of the river is catch-and-release only. One bank is in New Brunswick, the other in Quebec—but New Brunswick regulations prevail on both. There is no road along this part of the river, and you can easily forget about civilization. You'll often see moose along the banks. The pools are well marked and are easy to recognize. The river's numerous rapids can be tricky to negotiate during low water. More than once I've come very close to capsizing after getting stuck on rocks. There are also a few log jams to watch out for farther downriver. More grilse arrive later in the season, and also sea-run trout. Although this little river is only marginal (CPRD is 0.15), it is still one of my favorites. I can only hope things will improve.

The cabins on the Patapedia were generally included in the fee for the fishing rights, which are obtained from the MLCP. The Matapedia, Patapedia, and the Causapscal are now being administered by a local organization (similar to a ZEC) located in the town of Causapscal, Quebec, Tel. 418-756-5787 of 418-756-6174.

In 1989 I spent three days on the Quebec portion of the **Kedgewick**. Like the upper Patapedia, it is very small and wild. The fish are large but scarce (CPRD is 0.12). There are nice old-fashioned hunting cabins near the river, but it is a long drive over rough, dusty roads. It is quite a popular hunting area. I took a 10-pound (4.5-kilogram) salmon at Quigley Pool in 1991, and Richard hooked and lost a fish at La Roche. This section is run by a small outfitter based in Rimouski.

Most of my best fishing was at the Glen-Emma section of the **Matapedia** (CPRD 0.26). I fished it every year until I felt the prices had got out of hand. In 1984 the legendary Richard Adams was my guide. Richard is organized,

Scene of Gaspé fishing, as on the Patapedia.

methodical, expert with a canoe, and full of anecdotes and conversation. After an hour at Lower Murdock we had a 30-pounder (13.6 kilograms) on the bank, and Richard let out his trademark yell. That is my largest salmon to date.

The last year I fished the Matapedia was 1988. I had four days on the Glen-Emma Pool, one of them with Richard as my guide. The water was very low, and the fishing poor. We had Edgar's Pool in the morning and Richard's Pool in the afternoon. Things seemed hopeless, and I was ready to quit. It was nearly dark as I flogged the upper part of Richard's for the twentieth time or so. Richard was in conversation with a passer-by when my fly stopped. I thought I was stuck, and was ready to break off when a big salmon began thrashing at the surface. Suddenly my line went slack and I was sure it was off. Then the fish jumped upstream and I saw the line in its mouth. By the time we landed the fish, a 24-pounder (10.9 kilograms), it was quite dark. I'll never know how Richard managed to net it.

TABLE 11-7

CPRD of North Shore and Gaspé Rivers

River	1987–1991 Average	1992
Bonaventure	0.31	0.35
Godbout	0.36	0.32
Grand Cascapedia	0.25	0.39
Grand Trinité	0.25	0.14
Laval	0.10	0.07
Little Cascapedia	0.28	0.48
Matapedia	0.21	0.26
Moisie	0.29	0.28
Natashquan	1.24	1.22
Patapedia	0.13	0.15
Ste-Anne	0.31	0.21
Ste-Marguerite	0.17	0.19
York	0.21	0.28

Little more than an hour's drive from the Matapedia is the world-famous **Grand Cascapedia**, which flows down from its origins in the Shickshock Mountains and empties into the Baie des Chaleurs. This is a large river; most pools require canoes. Just looking at the pools will make your mouth water. The river holds large fish almost exclusively. An average catch is 20 pounds (9.1 kilograms), and 30-pounders (13.6 kilograms) are common. Salmon in the 40-pound range (18-plus kilograms) are caught every year, and grilse are almost unheard of. Most Atlantic-salmon rivers in the world pale in comparison.

Back in 1983, when I had just started salmon fishing, Claude Latraverse (whom I'd met on the Matapedia) took me to the wading pools of the upper Grand Cascapedia. Hardly anyone bothered with them then, and I was the only caller to request Pool 80. This pool is located on the Lake Branch, one of the two main tributary branches. The other is the Salmon Branch, which is a sanctuary. Pool 80, named *Montgomery*, is a 20-plus-minute drive on a dirt road.

The pool consists of a short rapid, a long middle section, and a small and disappointing tail. Pool 80 is a flash in the pan compared with some of the pools below, like Middle Camp, Murdock, or Big Curly's, but many of the fish do come up this branch to Pool 80 on their way to the spawning areas in the lake above.

Claude and I slept in our vans near the highway and drove down to the top of the logging road. The bugs were fierce that morning even though it was only mid-June. We started fishing early, and within a few hours we had two fish, a 20- and a 28-pounder (9.1 and 12.7 kilograms), on the bank. It was hard work carrying them out to the vans. My 44-inch (111-centimeter) male was a monster—at the time, the largest fish I had ever taken. I ached all over but I was happy.

The next day there was no action until noon, when I hooked another 28-pounder on a Magog Smelt Bucktail. I landed the fish, a female, in 10 minutes. Shortly thereafter, Claude latched into a 33-pounder (15 kilograms). The fish took two hours to land.

You can make reservations on the Grand Cascapedia by contacting the Société Cascapedia in Grand Cascapedia, telephone 418-392-5079. There is a mail-in lottery system for the guided pools, while the wading pools are allocated by an advance-phone-in system. Most of the river is privately owned. However, the private clubs—Englehards, Tracadie, Horse Island, and Middle Camp—may rent out fishing rights during slow periods.

Hardly a small river, the **Little Cascapedia** is only a short drive from its larger namesake, but is completely different. Its character changes continually. Some of its stretches are like glass—others are violent. Often it is wide, but at times exceedingly narrow. The rich-turquoise upper river gives way to emerald green, and finally to olive waters farther downstream. I've put in a canoe just above the Forks Pool and fished my way downriver toward St. Edgar. In addition to salmon, I've taken a number of sea-run trout to 2 pounds (0.9 kilogram) on a Magog Smelt Bucktail in the pool just above Melançon Camp.

Big Eddy and Millbrook are the best salmon pools on the river today. In 1981 I caught two fish my first day, a 14-pounder (6.4 kilograms) at Big Eddy and one of 18 pounds (8.2 kilograms) at Oxbow. I go back almost every year. On my last trip, in 1992 (an excellent year for the river), a 39-pound (17.7-kilogram) fish was taken from Big Eddy.

In recent years I have concentrated on Millbrook and Home Pool, both near the small town of St. Edgar. To reach Millbrook you must cross a cow pasture in the town; Home Pool is across from Camp Melançon. My best fish in Home Pool was a 20-pounder (9.1 kilograms); I took it early one morning on a size-6 Blue Charm.

There's considerable demand to fish the Little Cascapedia today. It's now run by a local club with a winter lottery system for half the rods; the others are available on a 48-hour advance draw. Part of the upper river is open to an unlimited number of rods. There are also the East and West branches, higher up, where no reservations are needed. These waters yield large sea-run trout as well as salmon.

Another excellent river in the vicinity is the **Bonaventure**. It's gin-clear and full of big rapids, and has a much larger run of salmon than the Little Cascapedia. I first fished the Bonaventure in 1983. My best fishing has been at Gros Saumon, which you can access from a dirt road half an hour or so out of the town of Bonaventure. There is a long staircase descending directly to the pool. Bonaventure salmon average only 10 pounds (4.5 kilograms), but a pool like Gros Saumon alone may contain several hundred fish. And there are always a few big salmon mixed in with the small ones. Many fish are lost in the strong rapids. On a good day, all rods on the limited-access section will catch fish. Unfortunately, this river's popularity has made it very difficult to get reservations through the winter lottery. However, there are very good pools in Section D that may be rented without advance reservations.

Yet another world-class river on the Gaspé is the **York**. The York passes through wilderness and mountain gorges before emptying into the ocean at the town of Gaspé. It wasn't until my fourth trip to the York that I landed one of its salmon, a 28-pounder (12.7 kilograms). It took my 2/0 Silver Rat at the end of my run through Gros Saumon and fought me for two hours in the fast water at the pool's tail.

One of the prettiest of the Gaspé rivers is the **Ste. Anne**. It is also one of my favorites, but it too is now very difficult to get passes for (a mail-in lottery started in 1994). Like some of the rivers flowing into the Baie des Chaleurs, the Ste. Anne originates in the Shickshock Mountains, but flows north instead of south. It is located in the Parc de la Gaspésie amid some of the most enchanting scenery in eastern Canada. This part of Quebec reminds me of Switzerland; the higher reaches of the mountains are capped white in July.

You can fish the Rivière Ste. Anne with guides and canoe in the upper section, or by wading in the lower section. There are lovely pools and spectacular scenery along most of the river. Runs have varied from year to year, but the Ste.

Anne boasts very large salmon. Twenty pounds (9.1 kilograms) is an ordinary catch, and 30- to 35-pounders (13.6 to 15.9 kilograms) are common. Early season is most unpredictable, but it is the nicest time to fish. The best pools on the upper section are Petit Sault and Ruisseau du Petit Volume, though in some years other pools like Cap Seize and Rivière à Marthe are very productive. Colonel, Cartier, and L'Islet 2 are also very good. The lower section of the Ste. Anne, which is still accessible by wading, boasts once-great pools like Petit Castor, L'Islet, and Wilson. Many have been filled in, but others such as Patate, Low, and Rets continue to produce many salmon. This part of the river can be accessed by a poorly maintained gravel road from St. Anne. Sadly, this part of the river has a reputation for heavy poaching. There is very little surveillance and many suspect that some of the residents along the river fish out of season. On the many occasions I have fished there I have never seen a warden, but I have had some unpleasant confrontations with locals.

In the decade I have fished for Atlantic salmon in Quebec and the Atlantic Provinces, I have seen enormous changes. Each year the fishing becomes more difficult, more expensive, and more competitive. Many of the camps—such as those on the Moisie and the Grand Cascapedia—have given up portions of their water. Ordinary anglers are willing to pay large sums of money for these beats, even in a difficult economy. But I understand this, because I know the excitement of casting a fly into a good pool.

The Rivers of Newfoundland and Labrador

by Len Rich

The island of Newfoundland and the mainland portion of the province, Labrador, lie on Canada's northeast coast. Newfoundland sits in the Atlantic Ocean, whose currents bring the entire North American Atlantic-salmon run close to its shores (Figure 1-4).

Immortalized by the films and writings of Lee Wulff, the rivers of Newfoundland and Labrador once teemed with salmon. More than 180 rivers in the province have been identified as salmon streams and are termed *scheduled waters*, open only for fly-fishing during the short summer months. Beginning in the mid-1960s, pressure from the commercial fishery slowly depleted stocks, particularly the larger multi-sea-year salmon, until by the late 1980s little remained in Newfoundland's rivers except sparse populations of grilse.

These depleted stocks forced Canada's Department of Fisheries and Oceans (DFO) to impose a five-year moratorium on the island's commercial salmon fishery. By the end of 1992 the vast majority of commercial fishermen had relinquished their licenses in return for a generous compensation package. A limited commercial fishery was permitted to continue for two Labrador zones—but with a reduced quota—due to its economic importance in that isolated region.

The commercial salmon ban in the Northern zone has led to a phenomenal resurgence of Newfoundland's rivers. For example, counting-fences on the **Gander River** showed triple returns during 1992—up to more than 22,000 grilse and salmon from the previous averages of 7,000 to 8,000 fish. The same is true of the **Exploits River**, the island's longest river system, which topped 20,000 fish counted in 1993, and has the potential to sustain annual runs of 100,000 salmon.

Newfoundland's third largest river, the **Humber**, experienced quality angling in both 1992 and 1993 as a result of the commercial ban. While there were no counting facilities, anglers reported excellent fishing—described as the best in 20 years. The genetic strain of large Lower Humber salmon, which may reach 40 pounds or more, appears stable. Other noted west-coast rivers—**Harry's**, **Serpentine**, the **Grand Codroy**, **Southwest Brook**, **Portland Creek**, **Robinsons**, **Torrent**, and **Ste. Genevieve**, to name only a few—also appear to be recovering from the ravages of commercial overfishing.

Improvement in Labrador's mainland has been slower. Biologists have noted a steady decline in large fish in Labrador's rivers, and abundance has not reached DFO's expectations. Exceptions are the **Pinware** and **Forteau Rivers** in the southern region, which are accessible by a ferry crossing from Newfoundland. Angling has improved there markedly since the commercial ban.

Conservation groups including the Atlantic Salmon Federation and its Regional Council, and the Salmoned Council of Newfoundland and Labrador, are calling for further reduced quotas. The situation was aggravated in 1993 by unseasonably hot weather and lower-than-normal water levels in most of Labrador's coastal rivers.

Accompanying the commercial ban was a reduced angling quota to eight grilse per angler per season, with a daily limit of one. There is also a complex system to determine when fish may be kept or when rivers are open only to catch-and-release; that is, one day you may be able to keep your fish, and the next

Newfoundland fishing scene.

day the same river may be no-kill. All salmon angling is fly-fishing only, and anglers are encouraged to use barbless hooks during no-kill periods. To fish Labrador you must keep abreast of all current local regulations.

In 1990 the province enacted new laws requiring all nonresident salmon anglers to utilize guide services when fishing on Newfoundland and on Labrador's mainland south of 52 degrees latitude (which includes the Forteau and Pinware Rivers). You may fish for trout without a guide within 800 meters (about a half-mile) of a provincial highway with a route designation, but you are prohibited from trout fishing in interior areas via woods roads unless you are accompanied by a licensed guide. Nonresidents who formerly lived in Newfoundland may fish in the company of a close relative, as outlined in the act.

Above 52 degrees north latitude, which includes the majority of Labrador, all nonresidents must utilize the services of an outfitter. This prevents the illegal access of nonresidents into remote areas by floatplane or other means. It also assures the safety of anglers in a sometimes-hostile environment.

Labrador abounds with outfitters that provide angling packages on a daily or weekly basis. Both on the mainland and on Newfoundland, outfitting is a highly competitive business, so in most cases you are assured of quality service. All outfitters are licensed annually by the provincial tourist department, which monitors and inspects each facility.

Outfitters' prices vary depending on length of stay and amenities provided (*all prices quoted below are in Canadian dollars*). For instance, rates on the **Gander River**—including guide, river boat, accommodations, and meals—are about $250 per day. Rates for remote island fly-in camps may exceed $2,000 per week. Due to remoteness, logistics, and high operating costs, a week's stay at an upper-end Labrador salmon lodge may approach $3,000, excluding air travel.

Anglers wanting a less-expensive trip to Newfoundland may stay in hotels, bed-and-breakfast establishments, or in one of the island's many campgrounds. You may hire guides on a daily basis. Costs vary between $75 and $100, and guides are limited to accompanying no more than two clients at a time. Locating a knowledgeable guide on short notice may be a problem, but lists are usually available at various wildlife and tourist offices.

Most Newfoundland rivers are small enough and shallow enough to wade (though you'll need chest waders). Two exceptions are the Lower Humber River and the Gander River, where anglers are advised to hire a boat as well as a guide to increase their safety and their chances of success.

Flies are available locally, and include sparse, moose-winged versions of English classics and patterns introduced from mainline rivers. Dark-bodied wet flies such as the Blue Charm are standard in all rivers, and other hair-winged patterns include the Thunder and Lightning, Green Highlander, Mar Lodge, Cosseboom, Silver Doctor, and Silver Tip. Popular dry-fly patterns include orange-hackled Buck Bugs, any of the Wulff series, MacIntosh, and Glitter Bugs of various colors. Small flies on hook sizes to 10 and 12 are necessary later in the season.

In 1993 a nonresident salmon license cost $50, which also permitted the angler to fish for trout. A current list of outfitters and angling regulations is available from the Provincial Tourism Department by calling their toll-free number: 800-563-6353.

Tourism publications offer a complete list of licensed outfitters, descriptions of each facility, list of amenities, type of angling available, and current prices. You should contact outfitters directly for detailed information.

THE RIVERS OF NOVA SCOTIA

by Bill Bryson

Nova Scotia has five major salmon rivers and 50 or more smaller ones. The five major ones are the Margaree on Cape Breton (covered separately by Dick Brown in the following section), the St. Mary's on the Eastern Shore, the Stewiacke in the Upper Bay of Fundy, and the LaHave and the Medway in southwestern Nova Scotia.

Renowned as a world-class stream, the **St. Mary's River** is composed of three sections: the main stem, and the east and west branches. In the first 12 miles(19 kilometers) from the sea, the main stem has 15 well-marked pools, all of which are wadeable.

The St. Mary's fishes well from mid-June through mid-September, but is known for its early run of large fish (15 to 30 pounds; 6.8 to 13.6 kilograms), which lasts through mid-July. A larger run of fish in the 4- to 12-pound (1.8- to 5.4-kilogram) class enters the system around July first. Most of these go up the west branch, but a few follow the large fish up the east. The 15 pools on the west branch and the 10 on the east are marked and are wadeable.

In the early season the best flies are large hairwings, with smaller ones used as the season progresses. Large Bombers are a must in the early season, with smaller ones coming to the fore later. Rods of 8 to 10 feet (2.4 to 3 meters) with 8- to 10-weight lines are the norm. Generally, 15-pound-test (6.8-kilogram) tippets are used early in the season, later lightening to 4- and 6-pound (1.8- and 2.7-kilogram) test.

The **LaHave River** also has two branches. About 90 percent of the fishing is done from their confluence at Pinehurst downstream to the town of Bridgewater. This 15-mile (24-kilometer) stretch has 15 well-marked, wadeable pools, which fish well from late May through mid-July. The north and east branches have a number of pools, but certain restrictions apply, so check

Nova Scotia fishing scene.

with Nova Scotia's Department of Natural Resources before fishing them. Hairwing flies in sizes 4 to 10 fished on 6- to 8-pound-test (2.7- to 3.6-kilogram) leaders, and 8- or 9-weight rods of 9 feet (2.7 meters) are the norm on the LaHave. The fish run 4 to 12 pounds (1.8 to 5.4 kilograms). Be sure to have Bombers and Buck Bugs in your fly box.

The **Medway River** is located some 30 miles (48 kilometers) west of the LaHave. Almost all fishing is between the upstream village of Greenfield and Mill Village at tidewater. There are 30 well-marked pools in this 12-mile (19 kilometers) stretch, and all are fished from boats. Fishing starts in May and runs through July, with peak times from May 20 through the end of June. The aforementioned fly patterns for the St. Mary's and the LaHave work well on the Medway. Hairwing dry flies in sizes 4 to 8 are very popular. The fish are mostly in the 4- to 12-pound (1.8- to 5.4- kilogram) range.

The **Stewiacke** is another of Nova Scotia's major rivers, and is one with a late run. The fish enter the river in late August and continue to run through

October. Best fishing is from September through October. The fish weigh from 4 to 16 pounds (1.8 to 7.3 kilograms). Most of the fishing is done from Upper Stewiacke to tidewater at East Stewiacke, a stretch of about 30 miles (48 kilometers) of wadeable water. A number of unmarked pools offer a challenge to adventuresome and perceptive salmon anglers. During high water, flies as large as 2/0 are used, and are replaced by sizes 4 and 6 as levels drop.

Nova Scotia's smaller rivers (spate rivers) are generally not suitable as primary locales for visiting anglers, as they are only productive after a substantial rain. However, at the right time they can be attractive secondary targets. Starting in Cape Breton, the **Middle** and **Baddeck Rivers** flow into the Bras d'Or Lakes, thence to the Atlantic. If you are fishing the fall run on the Margaree, you are in good position to take advantage of any rainy period that might bring fish into these streams. The pools—all wadeable—are not well marked, so I advise you to employ a guide for this side trip. The fish run from 10 to 30 pounds (4.5 to 13.6 kilograms).

The runs of the **Grand** and **North Rivers**, also located in Cape Breton, start earlier. The best fishing is in July, tapering off in August and September. The Grand flows from Loch Lomond Lake in Richmond County and enters the sea at the village of Grand River. It has a dozen or more pools that fish well after a rain. The 4- to 10-pound (1.8- to 4.5-kilogram) fish will take your St. Mary's flies well. The North River starts in northeast Victoria County and enters the ocean in St. Anns Bay at the North River Bridge. You can fish about 4 miles (6.4 kilometers) in the lower section, though you'll encounter rough terrain.

Rivers on the Eastern Shore include the **Salmon**, **Country Harbour**, **Liscombe** and **Ecum Secum**, all of which flow out of Guysborough County. The **Moser**, **Port Dufferin**, and the **East** and **West Rivers** reach Sheet Harbour. The **Musquodoboit** originates in Halifax County and flows into the Atlantic. They all have from six to 12 wadeable pools that fish well soon after a rain. The preferred flies are small: sizes 16 and 18 are not uncommon. They are presented with light rods (six to eight weight) with tippets of 3- to 6-pounds (1.4- to 2.7-kilogram) test. Fish run from 4 to 7 pounds (1.8 to 3.2 kilograms), except for the Musquodoboit, which can yield an occasional 20-pounder (9.1 kilograms).

Southwestern rivers include the **Gold**, the **Petite Rivière**, the **Clyde**, the **Roseway**, the **Tusket**, and the **Salmon**. The fish run from early June to mid-July, and are thus available to anglers concentrating on the LaHave and the Medway if they are prepared to make a substantial side trip.

For anglers whose primary target is the Stewiacke, we have these rivers that flow into Northumberland Strait: the **Phillip**, the **Wallace**, the **River John**, the **East River**, and the **West River**—all of which produce with the rising water levels of October.

Rivers flowing into the Bay of Fundy include the **Debert**, the **Salmon**, the **Folly**, the **Portapique**, the **Economy**, the **Ste. Croix**, the **Nictaux** and the **Annapolis**. The latter is a wadeable summer-run river that fishes best from mid-June to mid-July. The pools are accessible from roads on either side. They are not well marked, but the river offers a worthwhile challenge.

TABLE 11-8

CPRD of Nova Scotia Rivers, 1989 to 1992

River	1989	1990	1991	1992
Annapolis	0.07	0.13	0	0
Baddeck	0.56	0.45	0.43	0.33
Clyde	0.06	0	0.05	0.18
Country Harbour	0.28	0.29	0.32	0.09
Debert	0.23	0.04	b	a
Ecum Secum	0.22	0.12	0.05	0.14
Folly	0.24	0.12	b	a
Gold	0.22	0.16	0.08	0.13
Grand	0.15	0.19	0.08	0.11
LeHave	**0.27**	**0.22**	**0.10**	**0.15**
Liscomb	0.09	0.26	0.14	0.03
Margaree	**0.17**	**0.16**	**0.19**	**0.18**
Medway	**0.16**	**0.14**	**0.04**	**0.12**
Musquodoboit	0.15	0.14	0.13	0.12
Petite Riviére	0.21	0.21	0.08	0.19
River Herbert	0.75	0.06	b	a
Ste. Croix	0.18	0.05	0	a
Saint Mary's	**0.18**	**0.37**	**0.23**	**0.11**
Stewiacke	**0.27**	**0.08**	**0.29**	**a**
Tusket	0.13	0.13	0.09	0.14
Wallace	0.19	0.17	0.33	0.28
Waugh	0.11	0.37	0.48	0.28

a. River closed.
b. No angler reports.
Boldface type indicates major river.

TABLE 11-9

Total Catch on Five Nova Scotia Rivers

River	1983–1992 Average	1992
LaHave	1,942	1,202
Margaree	1,995	2,489
Medway	609	525
St. Mary's	1,288	436
Stewiacke	618	0

TABLE 11-10

Percent of Large Salmon[a] in the Catch of Various Nova Scotia Rivers, 1989–1992

River	1989	1990	1991	1992
LaHave	19	20	34	14
Margaree	74	70	70	74
Medway	26	19	49	9
St. Mary's	41	12	21	32
Stewiacke	14	19	0	b

a. Fish longer than 24.8 inches (63cm.)
b. River closed.

The CPRD of some of the rivers I've mentioned are given in Table 11-8. The five major streams of the province appear in bold type; the others are spate rivers (see Chapter 10). None of the major rivers showed any increase in fishing success in 1992 due to the Newfoundland net buyout. The explanation appears to be that while most areas had more-than-ample rainfall in 1992, there was a drought in northern and eastern Nova Scotia from mid- to late summer.

THE MARGAREE: NOVA SCOTIA'S BIG-FISH SALMON RIVER

by Dick Brown

The small, jewel-like Margaree produces more salmon than any river in Nova Scotia. Each year this stream's tally of angler-caught salmon surpasses the total taken on the LaHave, the Medway, the St. Mary's, and the Stewiacke *combined* (Table 11-9). Its exceptional salmon-to-grilse ratio—2.5:1—betters all but

Quebec's Moisie and Grand Cascapedia. In sheer numbers of fish and numbers of larger fish, the Margaree ranks among Canada's major salmon waters.

To veterans of wild, brawling salmon streams, the Margaree may at first appear too picturesque to hold so many big fish. Rising from the scenic Cape Breton Highlands, the river rushes down a hook-shaped course, plunging between small, rugged mountains. It then widens into a broad plain, twisting through storybook villages and farms until it reaches its mouth at Margaree Harbour on the province's northern coast.

Beginning in June, grilse and salmon enter the river from the North-umberland Strait. Grilse dominate the early runs, but salmon that have spent three or more years at sea enter the river throughout the warm months whenever the water is deep enough. This gives anglers a good chance at big fish all season long (Table 11-10).

Major runs of large fish occur in the autumn, when rainfall is heaviest. Experienced Cape Breton anglers consider September and October the best months.

The Northeast Branch, the river's main artery, offers fishing on over 40 pools. The uppermost pool, Cemetery, lies in the village of Inverness, just below a closed-water sanctuary that protects upriver spawning grounds. From Cemetery the river falls rapidly, coursing through a steep trough that skirts the base of Sugarloaf Mountain. Primary pools in this fast upper section are Sky Lodge, Ward's Rock, Bridge, and Black Rock.

The Northeast Branch continues south through a twisting canyon—site of Boar's Back, Jim Easter, Hatchery, Rock, and Ledge Pools. It then exits the narrow gorge, spilling into the farmlands of the Margaree Valley, where pools such as Red Bank, Cranton Bridge, Garden, Forks, and Big MacDaniel produce large numbers of fish.

A second branch of the river, the Southwest, enters the Margaree at Forks Pool. Flowing north from Lake Ainslie, the Southwest branch holds a dozen pools that produce well in the fall, including Gillis, Cameron's, and Noon.

General Fishing Information

Open season on the Margaree is June 1 to October 15. In recent years the lower 25 pools have remained open until October 31. A season nonresident salmon license cost $107 (*this and all prices listed below are in Canadian dollars*) in 1993. Anglers may keep up to 10 grilse under 63 centimeters (24.8 inches) during a season, but no more than two on a single day. Larger salmon must be released.

All licensed anglers may fish any pool in the nonsanctuary sections of the river, but access to many of them requires crossing private land. Close gates after you, carry out any litter, and avoid cultivated fields and grazing areas.

You may fish the Margaree on your own, but unless you are familiar with the river I suggest you hire a guide (approximately $120 per day) for the first few days to learn access to the pools and to orient yourself to the different sections of water. As pools change during the winter, most veterans fish with a guide for the first few days each year.

The Margaree Salmon Association (Margaree Forks, Cape Breton Island, Nova Scotia BOE 2AO) offers one of the best sources of information on the river. Members (annual fee $15) receive newsletters twice each season, and may attend the organization's annual meeting in October.

The best guidebook on the river, Jim Grey's *Handbook for the Margaree*, is available at the Margaree Salmon Museum in North East Margaree. Grey fully describes every major pool on the river, and most minor ones as well.

Flies and Fishing

Margaree anglers take fish on a variety of flies. The tight, steep banks of the river cause runoffs that raise the river high and fast. You may need wet flies as large as 2/0 and 3/0 during such spates. In low water, sizes 8 and 10 may be necessary. Among classic featherwing and hairwing patterns, favorites include the Black Bear-Green Butt, Jock Scott, Black Dose, Blue Charm, Thunder and Lightning, and the General Practitioner. Three local patterns produce well: the Ross Special, the Big Intervale Blue, and the Hospitality. Streamers such as the Mickey Finn and the Cardinelle also work well. Although the Margaree is not a noted dry-fly river, Bombers and Buck Bugs will take both salmon and grilse in low water.

Most veterans fish with standard 7- to 9-weight rods, but you'll see an occasional two-hander. Floating lines are common during normal water levels; sink-tip lines and even full-sink lines are used in heavy water. Flies must be tied on single or double hooks only, and may have no added weight. Although the occasional canoe drifts the river, transporting anglers from pool to pool, virtually all fishing is done by wading.

Accommodations

The Normaway Inn (902-248-2987) and the Big Intervale Salmon Camp (902-248-2275) offer full-service room and board. Housekeeping cabins include Cajun Cedar Log Cabins (902-248-2494), River Trail Cabins (902-248-2102),

Cranton Cottages (902-248-2985), and Chaisson's Riverview Cabins (902-235-2787). Heart of Hart's Tourist Farm (902-248-2765) and Buckles Motel (902-248-2053) both have cottages, rooms, and RV hookups.

Costs

If you fly to the Margaree, stay for a week at a full-service lodge, and fish with a guide every day, the total cost will run about $300 per day. Two anglers sharing a guide and room for a week can plan on spending about $200 per day—about average for Canadian salmon fishing.

To fish the Margaree less expensively, you can drive to Nova Scotia, stay in a housekeeping cabin, and fish with a guide for only four of the seven days. Cost for a single angler traveling alone would be about $200 per day. For two anglers sharing a cabin and guide, costs could be about $100 per day.

Travel

Flights from the United States arrive at both Halifax International and Sidney Airports. Driving time is an hour and a half from Sidney and four and a half hours from Halifax.

Driving from Boston takes 15 hours; from New York, 20 hours.

Guides
- Ed McCarty: 902-756-2442
- John Hart: 902-248-2578
- Fern Furey: 902-849-2204
- Eugene Le Blanc: 902-235-2024
- Ed Taylor 902-248-2244 (very good with beginners)

THE RIVERS OF MAINE

by Kenneth Beland[1]

Maine enjoys the distinction of being the only state in the country that provides recreational fisheries for Atlantic salmon. As a result of active restoration programs, Atlantic salmon are currently more abundant in Maine than at any time in the past 50 years. Salmon fisheries exist in at least 10 rivers, and anglers occasionally catch salmon on several other Maine rivers.

The average salmon caught by a Maine angler weighs approximately 9

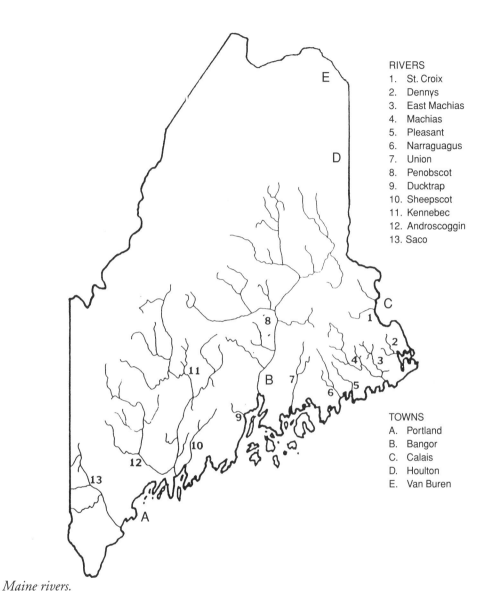

RIVERS
1. St. Croix
2. Dennys
3. East Machias
4. Machias
5. Pleasant
6. Narraguagus
7. Union
8. Penobscot
9. Ducktrap
10. Sheepscot
11. Kennebec
12. Androscoggin
13. Saco

TOWNS
A. Portland
B. Bangor
C. Calais
D. Houlton
E. Van Buren

Maine rivers.

pounds (4.1 kilograms) and has spent two years in the river and two years at sea before returning to spawn. Such salmon make up 85 to 90 percent of the rod catch in Maine rivers. Maine rivers also produce some very large salmon. The state record was caught in 1981 and weighed 28 pounds, 1 ounce (12.7 kilograms). Salmon weighing between 15 and 20 pounds (6.8 and 9.1 kilograms) are caught on several Maine rivers each year. These large salmon are on their second or third spawning migration, or have spent three years at sea. Grilse make up less than 10 percent of the catch.

When

The angling season for Atlantic salmon in Maine's inland waters extends from May 1 through September 15. The season extends through October 15 in the lower reaches of many rivers. Many tributary streams and areas near spring-fed brooks close to salmon angling on July 15. Waters of the Dennys River upstream of the narrows in Dennysville close to salmon angling on June 30.

Atlantic salmon may enter Maine rivers at any time between early May and late October. The peak salmon runs generally occur between Memorial Day and July 15. The timing of the run may vary slightly among individual rivers according to water conditions, but the best fishing normally occurs in June. September and October often provide some good fishing for Atlantic salmon as well. In general, salmon fishing is at its best when water temperatures are between 55 and 70 degrees F (12.7 and 21 degrees C). Salmon are less apt to strike a fly when temperatures exceed 70 degrees F.

Where

The **Penobscot River**, Maine's largest, boasts the largest Atlantic-salmon run of any river in Maine. In recent years, the run has varied from about 2,000 salmon to a high of 5,000 in 1986. The Penobscot also provides the most active sport fishery of any Maine salmon river. Recent catches have ranged from 600 to 1,000 salmon, about 75 percent of which are released. At present, there is a statewide bag limit of one salmon per person per year. Most Penobscot angling takes place in the half-mile (0.8 kilometer) of river downstream of a hydroelectric dam in Veazie, about 3 miles (4.8 kilometers) upstream of Bangor. Most anglers opt for such well-known and proven pools as the Eddington, Dickson, Wringer, Beach, and Guerin pools, as well as the Bangor Water District pipeline between Eddington and Veazie. This section of river is fished from both banks as well as by boat. During May, salmon are also taken from the Bangor Salmon Pool, which is best accessed from the Penobscot Club in Brewer.

Many miles of potentially productive salmon water lie upstream of the defunct Veazie Dam. Exploring waters between Howland and Dover-Foxcroft,

Maine fishing scene.

or in the Mattawaumkeag area (about 50 miles or 80 kilometers upstream), often pays dividends to an adventurous angler. Salmon are usually taken in upriver areas in July and August.

The **Narraguagus River** may be the best known of the smaller salmon rivers in Maine. It flows through the town of Cherryfield, located about 50 miles (80 kilometers) east of Bangor along U.S. Route 1. The river provides an average rod catch of about 75 salmon per year. The most popular pools are located in Cherryfield. About half the catch occurs in the Cable Pool, where anglers take turns fishing rotation downstream. Other good pools in Cherryfield include the Maples, Stillwater, Railroad Bridge, and Gull Rock.

Salmon are also taken at the Tidal Falls in Millbridge, about 5 miles (8 kilometers) south of Cherryfield. For those seeking solitude, a hike into Little Falls or a canoe trip between Deblois and Cherryfield, may prove a memorable fishing experience. The best fishing on the Narraguagus usually occurs between Memorial Day and July 4, although a few salmon are occasionally taken during September and early October.

The estuaries of the **Machias** and **East Machias Rivers** join near the town of Machias (80 miles east of Bangor on Route 1). Each river supports a self-sustaining run of Atlantic salmon. The Machias is the larger of the two rivers, and generally has the larger run. Pools are scattered throughout the lower 30 miles (48 kilometers) of the river, and fishing generally peaks between June 15 and July 15. Water levels on the Machias are usually quite stable, so the fishery is less dependent upon regular rainfall. Popular fishing sites on the Machias River include the Point Pool, Money Island, the Railroad Bridge, and Munson's Pitch, all located in the Machias-Whitneyville area.

Pools farther upstream include Great Falls, Holmes Falls, the Wigwam Rapids, and Little Falls. Access to these and other upriver areas is primarily by logging roads. Finding some of the sites may be difficult without first obtaining good directions. Catches on the East Machias River are approximately half as large as those from the main river. Catches on the East Machias average about 40 Atlantic salmon per year.

The East Machias River also provides a bonus of landlocked salmon up to 4 pounds (1.8 kilograms) to a few lucky anglers. Most Atlantic salmon on the East Machias River are caught between Memorial Day and July 4. In contrast to the Machias River, nearly all the fishing on the East Machias occurs in its lower 3 miles (4.8 kilometers), in the town of East Machias. Productive sites include the Gaddis Pool, the Jacksonville Pool, and the Berry Pool. Anglers occasionally have success fishing the rips in the middle reaches of the river as well. Those sites are best accessed by canoe, though logging roads pass close to some pools. The **Dennys River** is the easternmost river in Maine with a self-sustaining salmon run. It enters Cobscook Bay in Dennysville, about 100 miles (161 kilometers) east of Bangor along Route 1. Salmon numbers have been low in recent years, with catches of 5 to 25 fish per year. Success on this relatively small river depends on water levels. The timing of the Dennys salmon run is somewhat more erratic than on Maine's larger rivers. Salmon fishing on the Dennys peaks in late June and early July, though summer rainstorms can bring on brief flurries of activity in July and August. Productive pools on the lower river include Charlie's Rip, the Community Pool, the Ledge Pool, and the Dam Pool. Farther upstream lie Trestle and Dodge Pools. Those willing to hike or canoe often find success at other such sites as Little Falls or Long Point.

The Ste. Croix River forms the international boundary between Maine and New Brunswick, and is the site of international efforts to restore a run of Atlantic salmon. Current regulations on this river prohibit the taking of salmon longer than 25 inches (63.5 centimeters), though you may keep one fish (grilse) of this length or less. The fishery on the Ste. Croix is quite new, and many potentially productive sites have yet to be discovered. Nearly all the fishing presently takes place in the Calais, Maine-St. Stephen, New Brunswick area, especially the waters downstream of the Milltown hydroelectric dam.

Some of the rivers in central and southern Maine provide limited fishing for Atlantic salmon. The **Sheepscot River** flows through the town of Wiscasset, about 40 miles (64 kilometers) east of Portland. The run on this river is relatively small, and the catch averages only about 10 fish per year. Popular angling sites include the Tidal Falls and Larrabee Pool—both located in Alna—as well as a number of smaller pools scattered along the river's length. The run may take place through summer and early fall, depending on water levels. The **Ducktrap River** enters Penobscot Bay at Lincolnville Beach, about 50 miles (80 kilometers) south of Bangor. This is the smallest river in Maine that provides salmon fishing. Salmon typically enter the river in September and October, and anglers catch up to 20 salmon per year from two tidewater pools.

Atlantic salmon restoration efforts on the **Saco River** have provided a limited sport fishery in the Biddeford-Saco area. Officials anticipate that sportfishing opportunities will improve here as restoration progresses.

There are presently no Atlantic-salmon restoration programs on the Kennebec and Androscoggin Rivers, yet anglers on those rivers take a few salmon in most years. The salmon that enter those rivers are predominantly strays from other rivers, although a few salmon are naturally spawned in tributary streams.

How

Fly-fishing is the only method by which Atlantic salmon may be taken in Maine rivers. Anglers seeking Atlantic salmon in inland waters must possess both an Atlantic-salmon license and an inland-fishing license. Anglers in designated coastal waters need only have an Atlantic-salmon license. License fees are published in the regulations folder.

The daily and seasonal bag limit in Maine is one Atlantic salmon. Released fish do not count. Special regulations further limit the number of salmon longer than 25 inches (63.5 centimeters) that may be taken from some rivers. It's wise to consult the regulations folder to determine the special regulations for certain rivers. All Atlantic salmon taken by anglers in Maine must be immediately tagged (tags are provided with the license) and registered at designated stations.

Flies

Perhaps no subject stirs as much debate among salmon anglers as that of which fly to use. Certain flies, however, have become standard on nearly all Maine rivers. Among wet flies, the Cosseboom, the Rusty Rat, and the Black Bear flies (with green, red, or orange butts) may be found in nearly any angler's vest. On the Penobscot, several patterns developed by local tyers have become popular, including the Wringer, the Verdict, and the Pink Ent.

Dry flies are also effective on Maine Atlantic salmon. Perhaps the most popular pattern of all is the Bomber. The Butterfly is another effective pattern. It may be fished dry, wet, or dragged through the surface film. The Wulff series of dry flies have proven themselves for many years, especially the White Wulff. Many lesser-known, or homemade patterns are also effective.

Scotland's South Esk

by Bill Cummings

As a trout angler, I was always interested in salmon fishing, and hoped someday to "graduate" to it. To prepare, I read everything I could find on the subject. The majority of the books I read were British, and dealt extensively with the great salmon waters of Scotland—rivers such as the Tay, the Tweed, and the Spey.

So it was I found myself one day, in the fall of 1960, browsing through the fly shop of Mr. J.S. Sharpe in downtown Aberdeen. I had business in Europe, and had arranged to remain in Scotland for several days before proceeding to the Continent.

J.S. Sharpe's was stocked with all the latest equipment and fashions for the European fly-fisher. It had an excellent line of split-bamboo fly rods, and at the time was Europe's only source of resin-impregnated bamboo rods. It was there I saw for the first time split-bamboo rods that had no ferrules. Instead, the rod's two sections were cut at a long bias, and were joined by wrapping them tightly with tape. This eliminated any dead spot in the rod's action, the clerk explained—a shortcoming of the metal ferrules of the day. And if wrapped prop-

Scots fishing scene.

erly, there was no chance the rod would come apart while fishing.

On learning I was a Yank, the clerk asked if I would like to go upstairs and see the fly-tying table. I imagined a small tying bench with which the owner and his clerks occupied their slow times. To my surprise, the staircase opened onto a large room furnished with a round table of about ten feet in diameter, at which were seated a number of women of all ages. Each was tying a full-dress salmon fly. Centered on the table was a large lazy Susan brimming with materials, revolving almost continuously as the women tied. As soon as the fly's head was dry, the tyer placed it into a box next to her. These were part-time employees, the clerk said, often housewives, who worked only a few hours each day. They were paid daily according to the number of flies they'd dressed. He handed me a fly to examine. The quality was impressive, especially considering how quickly it had been tied.

When we returned to the salesroom the clerk introduced me to Mr. Sharpe, who asked if I intended to do any fishing during my stay. At the time my salmon experience was minimal. I'd spent some time on New Brunswick's Miramichi, and on the Machias in Maine. But for years I'd envisioned myself on a Scottish river.

The local river, the Don, which flows through the outskirts of Aberdeen and enters the North Sea, was over its banks due to recent heavy rains. Fly-fishing would be impossible, Mr. Sharpe said, and suggested the South Esk, some hundred miles to the south. A smaller river, it might be in better shape. He confirmed this with a phone call. The outfitter on this river, Mr. Phillips, leased the local laird's castle at Bridge O'Dun for salmon fishing and bird hunting, and could put me up overnight. Mr. Phillips could rent me a rod, said Mr. Sharpe, but he did not rent waders. Mr. Sharpe insisted I take a pair of his with me and leave them there when I was through. He would be visiting Bridge O'Dun within a week, and would pick them up then.

The next morning I took the train south to Montrose, and as arranged by Mr. Sharpe, was met on the station platform by a woman driving an MG. She was there to meet her husband, who was coming north from London for some grouse hunting. When the woman's husband arrived presently, we packed our luggage tightly into the MG and drove the few miles to the castle.

When we arrived, the grouse hunt was about to get underway. Hunters were going up and down the broad staircase, shouting to each other about guns, ammunition, beaters, clothing, lunches, and a hundred other things. I finally located Mr. Phillips in the kitchen, where he had his hands full with an irate old man who didn't like the lunch that had been packed for him. After Mr. Phillips repacked the man's lunch and sent him on his way, he turned to me and said, "The old coot will be back here by ten o'clock and eat a hot lunch in the dining room."

Mr. Phillips explained that in addition to the water controlled by the laird, which was some distance away, there were a number of other pools that could be reached by automobile. As I had no transportation, he asked his only other fishing guest, a retired air commodore, to take me along with him.

After breakfast Mr. Phillips handed me my rod—a two-handed weapon of some 14 feet, mounted with a Hardy reel that looked as though it could've docked the Queen Mary— and a box of flies, none of which I could identify. The commodore and I drove off down a narrow gravel road through fields and patches of woods, eventually stopping at a railroad crossing whose gates were down. The commodore shut the engine off, and we waited. Through the gate-house windows I could see the gatekeeper, but more than ten minutes passed with no sign of movement—either from him *or* of an approaching train. I suggested to the commodore that he sound his horn. That would do nothing, he explained, except make our wait 20 minutes longer

After several more minutes, the gatekeeper finally stirred.

Where we parked our car on the South Esk, the river was hardly larger than a good-sized trout stream. We set up our rods, and had just arrived at our first pool when we heard the puttering of a small engine. "Damn, it's the bailiff!" the commodore cried. "If he gets talking we shall lose half the morning's fishing."

Riding a motorized bicycle, the bailiff drew up alongside us and stopped, then dismounted and painstakingly propped the bike up on its stand. He carefully examined the commodore's fishing license, then asked me for mine.

"Look here, my good man," the commodore said sternly, "this chap is an American, and is here only for a few hours. To ask him to take out a license for such a short time is not to show proper appreciation for a valiant ally during the recent war."

The bailiff muttered something about the validity of the law and his duty to protect the river—but most of this was lost on the commodore, who had plunged ahead to the first pool.

At first the two-handed rod seemed awkward, but once I got the timing down I found it cast efficiently, and with much less effort than I'd supposed. As I learned, almost all fishing in Scotland is done from the bank, with rarely any room for a back cast. This makes *spey casting* a necessity. A spey cast is a modified roll cast during which you load the rod twice—once on your left side and again on your right—so that your line describes a figure eight in flight.

The day had begun cool and damp, and now it started to rain. We had covered a half-dozen pools with no action when the skies really opened up. "Look," the commodore said, "you are shaking like a leaf and you appear to be wet through. Let's go back to the castle and warm up. I have a heater in my room."

I felt better after shedding my wet clothes and getting into some dry ones. Fortunately I'd brought along two sweaters. The interior walls of the old castle were stone, wet with condensation. The portraits of the laird's ancestors adorning the hallways showed generations of hard-bitten expressions—no doubt from the weather.

The commodore had inherited a good section of the River Tay from his father's estate. On retiring from the RAF he decided to lease out the water and use the proceeds to finance his fishing on a number of other rivers. We got to talking about the differences between fishing in Scotland and North America. I noticed that the feeble fire in the fireplace had all but gone out, and I could feel the damp cold penetrating my bones. I asked him if it might not be a good time to get out the heater he had spoken of while we were on the river. By all means, he said, and fetched a bottle of Scotch and two glasses. Our discussion continued through dinner, though it was difficult to hear over the roar of the grouse hunters. They evidently had their own heaters.

Twice more, when I had business in Europe, I set aside a few days to visit Bridge O'Dun. Both times I arrived in June, when the sun stayed on the water until 8:30 in the evening, and you could fish until nearly 11:00. I brought my own flies with me, and found that the Cosseboom worked quite well. The Scots were impressed, and planned to dress some of their own the following season.

Mr. Phillips insisted I kill any fish I landed; he said he would sell it to the local market and subtract the price from my bill. The only fish of any size I hooked went a bit over 20 pounds (9.1 kilograms), but it was a disappointing fight. After a couple of turns around the pool, the fish allowed me to bring it to net in less than 15 minutes. No complaints, however, with the amount its sale reduced my bill.

Mr. Phillips was a great believer in small tube flies fitted with a size-16 treble hook and fished right on the surface. He gave me some to try, and they took fish well. I even took a few later on the Matane using small single hooks, but they certainly were not as effective as they were with the trebles.

For information on salmon fishing in Scotland, contact the British Tourist Authority, 40 West 57th Street, New York, NY 10019-4001, Tel. 212-581-4700.

NOTE

1. Reprinted from *Maine Fish & Wildlife* with the permission of Maine's Atlantic Sea Run Salmon Commission.

Appendices

APPENDIX A

ESTIMATING WEIGHT

In Chapter 8 I wrote that the longer a salmon is out of water after you land it, the greater are its chances of dying after you release it. Before catch-and-release, dead salmon were weighed, and the numbers entered into camp records as evidence of the angler's prowess. When catch-and-release became widespread there was a need for an expedient method to obtain the weight of the fish before releasing them—at least among anglers who kept score.

THE SALMOMETER

You can quickly estimate a salmon's weight by measuring the fish's length, then referring to the compilation in Table A-1, which was reached by averaging the weight of all salmon of a given length captured over a number of years (Atlantic Salmon Federation Salmometer). As salmon of the same length may vary widely in girth, your estimate is only a rough approximate.

TABLE A-1

Estimates of Salmon Weight From Length Measurements

Length (inches)[a]	Weight (pounds)[b]	Length	Weight	Length (inches)[a]	Weight (pounds)[b]
19	2.7	31	11.6	43	28.7
20	3.1	32	12.4	44	30.3
21	3.4	33	13.7	45	31.8
22	4.2	34	15.2	46	33.3
23	5.0	35	16.7	47	34.8
24	5.8	36	18.2	48	36.3
25	6.6	37	19.7	49	37.8
26	7.4	38	21.2	50	39.3
27	8.2	39	22.7	51	40.8
28	9.0	40	24.2	52	42.3
29	9.8	41	25.7		
30	10.7	42	27.2		

a. All lengths to be measured on perpendiculars from end of the snout to end of the middle rays of the tail.
b. Data from the Salmometer courtesy of the Atlantic Salmon Federation.

The Ward and Sturdy Formulae

Edward R. Hewitt (1950) credits William H. Ward with this equation to estimate a salmon's weight from its length and girth:

$$W = Z \times l \times g^2$$
where,
W = weight in pounds
l = length in inches
g = girth in inches
Z = 0.00125.

The Sturdy Formula is the same, except that Z = 0.00133. It is thought to be more accurate than the Ward equation to estimate the weight of a steelhead trout.

APPENDIX B

THE BIGGEST FISH

While fishing the Cross Point Pool of the Restigouche River, New Brunswick, in June of 1990, Ken Jamieson hooked an enormous salmon. It took a size-4 Silver Rat tied on a double hook. An hour and a quarter later Jamieson landed the fish, measured its length and girth, and then released it. With a length of 68.5 inches (174 centimeters) and a girth of 29 inches (73.6 centimeters), the Ward Formula estimated the fish's weight at 72 pounds (32.6 kilograms). The Sturdy Formula estimated it at 77 pounds (34.9 kilograms). Since the fish could not be officially weighed, it did not qualify as a record by the International Game Fish Association. The official IGFA fly-rod world record for Atlantic salmon stands at 47 pounds (21.3 kilograms).

Both the Ward and Sturdy formulae assume the fish's volume can be calculated by approximating its shape by a combination of two cones and a cylinder. Multiplying by the known density of salmon gives the weight as a function of length and girth. When these estimates are compared against the actual scale weights, the Ward Formula is found to be as much as 20.5 percent low, while the Sturdy may be as much as 26 percent high. The Salmometer's estimate is almost always too low; in one case by as much as 30 percent.

WEIGHING THE NET

I fear the increased time the salmon must remain out of water for us to make all these measurements results in our subjecting it to unnecessary stress, which may threaten its survival. The safest and most accurate way to weigh a fish is to net the fish (using a net whose bag is made from knotless cotton mesh), quickly weigh the full net, then subtract the weight of the net from your total. This yields an accurate weight while causing minimal harm to the fish.

GLOSSARY

alevin—A hatchling salmon during its first few weeks of life. Alevins are characterized by their attached yolk sacs, which the young fish utilize as nourishment.

baggot—A female salmon that has not been able to spawn and reabsorbs her eggs. Also called a *rawner*.

bright fish—A silver-colored salmon ascending the river on its spawning run. It will darken in color as it approaches the spawning beds.

bulging—Activity of a fish that disturbs the water's surface but does not break it.

chugging—Action of a hooked salmon, usually a cockfish, whereby it descends to the river bottom and shakes its head to throw the hook.

classic fly—Elaborately dressed salmon fly used in the nineteenth and early to mid-twentieth century. Classic flies utilize exotic feathers in complex combinations. They are seldom fished today, but are prized as things of beauty and epitomize the fly-tyer's art.

CPRD (Catch Per Rod Day)—A statistical measure of fishing success obtained by dividing the total number of fish caught on a river or a section of river by the number of days the anglers who caught them (or tried to) spent fishing.

cutting—The henfish's tail action by which she clears a depression in the redd (the spawning bed) to deposit her eggs.

dangle—A wet fly is considered to be "dangling" or "in the dangle" after it completes its swing and is holding in the current directly downstream.

drop—The distance a fishing canoe moves downstream between the angler's casting sequences.

fingerling—Life stage of a salmon after it attains a length of 1 inch (2.5 centimeters) and before it exceeds the length of a finger.

fry—Immature salmon that have just emerged from the gravel in which they hatched. The life stage between alevin and fingerlings.

grilse—A salmon (most often a male) that returns to its natal river after only one winter at sea. Legally defined in Canada as a fish not exceeding 63 centimeters (24.8 inches) in length, measured from the tip of its snout to the fork of its tail.

gut (silkworm gut)—Leader material used prior to the invention of nylon monofilament. It was gleaned from silkworms by removing the silk-producing gland of the insect and drawing its contents through dies of various diameters. Gut leaders could not be used until they had been first soaked in water.

hairwing fly—Salmon fly using animal hair for its wings—sometimes as substitutes for rare or illegal feathers used in classic patterns. Bucktail and squirrel tail, as well as the body hair from bears and foxes are only a few of the hairs used.

jigging—Foul-hooking a salmon with a large heavy hook, usually a double or treble. Jigging is illegal in virtually all Atlantic salmon waters.

kelt—A salmon that has survived spawning and is making its way back to the sea. Also known as a *black salmon.*

killick—A canoe anchor, often a stone or a length of heavy chain.

kype—A hooklike prolongation of the male salmon's lower jaw that develops prior to spawning.

lie—An area in a pool the salmon uses to rest between moves upriver. A lie must provide a good flow of well-oxygenated water, but require minimal energy for the salmon to hold its position. Unimpeded access to deep water is also essential.

mending—A procedure used to prevent drag when fishing across water whose current speed is uneven. For example, when fishing across fast water into slower water, immediately after casting you would lift the line free of the surface, swinging upriver and a bit forward to deposit it in an upstream arc. This mend will delay the fly's cross-current acceleration until the fast water bows the line. Also, a kelt that has returned to the sea and has started feeding is said to be mending.

parr—The salmon's riverine life stage for the two or more years between the fingerling stage and its change to a smolt. Parr are characterized by a series of eight to 11 dark blotches on either side of their body.

pond—A section of river where the water is so slack that the salmon will not pause in it for any significant length of time at normal water levels.

porpoising—Surface activity of a salmon similar in appearance to that of porpoises. That is, as the fish moves forward, its head breaks the water's surface, and as it dives, you get a glimpse of its tail as well.

Portland Creek riffling hitch—Fly attachment whereby you take two half hitches with the leader behind the head of the fly after tying it on with a regular knot. When fished, a riffle-hitched fly skitters across the water's surface on its side, which salmon sometimes find attractive.

redd—The salmon's spawning bed, in which the female has cleared a depression with her tail.

rotation—A system that allows a group of anglers to have an equal chance on a pool, usually in public water. The anglers proceed down the pool in an order chosen by lot, taking a step after each cast. Once they reach the tail, the anglers return to the head of the pool. Rules vary concerning raised fish that are not hooked.

running—In the general sense, *running* means there are a good number of fish in the river; whence we get the phrase "The run is on." In a more restricted sense it refers to the salmon's upstream movement. Running usually occurs during periods of good flow and/or low light—often at night.

shingle—An area of exposed rock or gravel between the water's edge and the high-water mark.

showing—An act by which the salmon reveals its presence, usually by breaking the surface or jumping clear of the water.

skitter—To move a fly across the surface.

smolt—The stage of river life succeeding the parr stage, during which time the fish undergoes physiological changes that adapt it for ocean life.

spate—A flood of water brought on by rain.

sport—Term used by a guide to identify his client. Abbreviation of *sportsman*.

stale fish—A fish that has taken the entire summer to migrate upriver. Stale fish are dark, and are usually difficult to catch.

stock—No two rivers provide exactly the same environment for salmon, and each river develops a strain of salmon peculiarly adapted to its conditions. This strain constitutes the river's stock.

swim—The movement of the wet fly through the water.

tailer—Mechanical device for landing salmon consisting of a noose of braided wire that is slipped over the fish's tail and tightened.

BIBLIOGRAPHY

Anderson, Gary J. 1985. *Atlantic salmon and the fly fisherman.* Toronto: Doubleday.

Anderson, Gary J. 1990. *Atlantic salmon fact and fantasy.* Montreal: Salar Publishing.

Ashley-Cooper, John. 1983. *A line on salmon.* London: H. F. & G. Witherby.

Bashline, L. James. 1987. *Atlantic salmon fishing.* Harrisburg, Pa.: Stackpole.

Bates, Joseph D. Jr. 1970. *Atlantic salmon flies and fishing.* Harrisburg, Pa.: Stackpole.

Buck, Richard. 1993. *Silver swimmer: The struggle for survival of the wild Atlantic salmon.* New York: Lyons & Burford.

Calcott, Ian. 1963. *The art of salmon fishing.* London: Oliver & Boyd.

Dube, Jean-Paul. 1983. *Salmon talk.* Clinton, N.J.: Amwell.

Falkus, Hugh. 1984. *Salmon fishing: A practical guide.* London: H. F. & G. Witherby.

Fulsher, Keith and Charles Krom. 1981. *Hair-wing Atlantic salmon flies.* Berlin, N.H.: Fly Tyer, Inc.

Gingrich, Arnold. 1966. *The well-tempered angler.* New York: Knopf.

Graesser, Neil. 1985. *Fly fishing for salmon.* Washington, D.C.: Stone Wall Press.

Green, Philip P. M. 1984. *New angles on salmon fishing.* London: George Allen & Unwin.

Hasler, Arthur D. and Allan T. Scholz. 1983. *Olfactory imprinting and homing in salmon.* New York: Springer-Verlag.

Hewitt, Edward Ringwood. 1950. *A trout and salmon fisherman for seventy-five years.* New York: Scribner's.

Hutton, John E. 1949. *Trout and salmon fishing.* Boston: Little, Brown.

Jennings, Preston J. 1935. *A book of trout flies.* New York: Crown.

Jones, J. W. 1959. *The salmon.* New York: Harper & Brothers.

Jorgenson, Poul. 1978. *Salmon flies.* Harrisburg, Pa.: Stackpole.

Kelson, George. 1895. *The salmon fly.* London: published by the author, c/o Messrs. Wyman & Sons.

Knowles, Derek. 1987. *Salmon on a dry fly*. London: H. F. & G. Witherby.

LaBranche, George M.L. 1951. *The salmon and the dry fly*. New York: Scribner's.

LaFontaine, Gary. 1990. *The dry fly: New angles*. Helena, Mont.: Greycliff Publishing.

Netboy, Anthony. 1968. *The Atlantic salmon: A vanishing species?* Boston: Houghton Mifflin.

Oglesby, Arthur. 1986. *Fly fishing for salmon and sea trout*. Ramsbury: Crowood Press.

Russell, Jack. 1951. *Jill and I and the salmon*. Boston: Little, Brown.

Scott, Jock. 1982. *Greased line fishing for salmon*. Portland, Ore.: Frank Amato Publications.

Sosin, Mark and Bernard Kreh. 1991. *Practical fishing knots II*. New York: Lyons & Burford.

Stewart, Clayton. 1986. *Life on the Miramichi*. Woodstock, N.B.: Carleton Printing.

Stewart, Clayton. 1990. *Recollections*. Fredericton, N.B.: Unipress.

Stewart, Dick. 1986. *The hook book*. Intervale, N.H.: Northland Press.

Taverner, Eric. 1948. *Salmon fishing*. Woodstock, Vt.: Countryman Press.

Trench, Charles Chenevix. 1974. *A history of angling*. Chicago: Follett Publishing.

Weeks, Edward. 1968. *Fresh waters*. Boston: Little, Brown.

Weeks, Edward. 1984. *The Miramichi fish and game club: A history*. Fredericton, N.B.: Brunswick Press.

Wulff, Lee. 1983. *The Atlantic salmon*. Piscataway, N.J.: Winchester Press.

INDEX